Failure Modes to Failure Codes

John Reeve and Derek Burley

Failure Modes to Failure Codes

John Reeve and Derek Burley

ISBN 978-1-941872-74-1
HF012020

Printed in the United States of America.

Publisher: Reliabilityweb, Inc.

Design and Layout: Apolonia Lemus
Developmental Editor: Robert Weinstein

For information: Reliabilityweb.com
www.reliabilityweb.com
8991 Daniels Center Drive, Suite 105, Ft. Myers, FL 33912
Toll Free: 888-575-1245 | Phone: 239-333-2500
E-mail: crm@reliabilityweb.com

10 9 8 7

Table of Contents

Foreword

For too many years, organizations using CMMS products have struggled to capture accurate failure data. Failure modes—the language of RCM—seem to have gotten lost in the shuffle. Validated failure data is especially important for those wanting to make more informed decisions regarding their worst offenders. *Failure Modes for Failure Codes* describes a holistic solution that encompasses failure mode capture on the Work Order, failure analytic design, and the role of the reliability team in performing chronic failure analysis.

In most asset intensive industries, it is the recurring failures that predominantly drive O&M cost. According to reliability expert Charles Latino, 40–60% of all maintenance costs are due to chronic failures. If that is true, shouldn't the CMMS be focused on failure data capture and analysis? Without validated failure data capture, you only have a Work Order ticket system. Every day that goes by, this is lost failure history, never to be recovered.

Taking somewhat of a reverse engineering approach, analytical reports should drive the design of the CMMS. A failure report mock-up may be all that is initially required. Once the report design is known, administrators can identify the necessary data input fields, as well as roles required to support the failure analysis process. Later, when resources permit, the report can be coded and released.

New CMMS users should not assume the failure analytic they need will exist out of the box. In addition, it is highly probable that the Work Order entry screen does not support failure mode capture. The next question will be, "Can the software be configured?" The primary requirements you should be looking for are:

1. Ability to configure—you must be able to add fields to screens (or to the database) if necessary.

2. Knowledge to configure—you must understand what needs to be configured (e.g., vision).
3. Authority to configure—you must have authorization from the administrators to configure.

Most practitioners agree that RCM is the best method for determining maintenance tactics. If properly configured, the CMMS can support RCM. All that is really required is a vision for operational excellence.

Leveraging data to make more informed decisions should be the primary objective behind any enterprise management system. You can put volumes of data into a CMMS, but it needs to have a purpose beyond creating Work Orders and entering actuals.

Best-in-class organizations know how to leverage data within the CMMS. They also understand which strategies help them become more proactive. Chronic failure analysis offers the best chance to identify bad actors and manage recurring problems. Quite simply, there's not enough time in the day to track all of the assets. The best approach is to focus on the significant few that have the majority of problems—also called managing by exception. This technique involves consolidating and aggregating data on similar fields to see which value has the highest occurrence. The next question becomes, "What fields should we use for grouping?" There could be multiple fields and some are better than others. But, trying to reduce reactive maintenance by focusing on Work Order counts or total cost is not that meaningful.

All too often failure analysis is based on 1) tribal analysis, 2) narrative text fields, or, in some cases, 3) a formal root cause analysis (RCA). All three methods are used once the asset has failed. At the end of the day, the equipment is in charge, meaning the staff reacts when failure occurs.

Many organizations jump all too quickly to time-based preventive maintenance strategies as the primary–and only–technique to prevent failures. A better approach is to determine strategies based on formal failure analysis. The goal is to link every maintenance strategy to a failure mode that you are trying to prevent. Reliability centered maintenance, or RCM analysis, is a proven technique to help define the failure modes and suggested maintenance tactics. A similar technique is called PMO, or preventive maintenance optimization.

In addition to RCM/PMO analysis, there is a technique called defect elimination. It involves a cross-functional team that focuses on a critical system, looking for all types of defects and attempts to implement corrective action sooner than later. By eliminating the defect up front, the failure will (ideally) never occur.

One method more valuable than any of the above is called chronic failure analysis. With this approach, stakeholders can focus on the significant few and drill down into the root cause. The ideal group by fields include operational downtime, asset condition, and actual costs divided by replacement cost. Actionable data in this format helps empower the reliability team to make informed decisions and manage by exception. Chronic failure analysis doesn't need to wait for a failure event. Rather, it analyzes failure modes of the worst offenders to support continuous improvement of maintenance strategies.

Figure F-1 illustrates several innovative ideas that make this approach unique: 1) the creation of a Pareto-style failure analytic, 2) the setup of a reliability team, 3) a clear understanding of failure mode, 4) capture of the failure mode on the Work Order, (5) capture of the asset condition, (6) formalization of the Work Order feedback, and (7) storage of RCM analysis results directly inside the CMMS.

This concept uses Pareto analysis to identify the worst offenders and then drill down on failure modes.

You can install/implement a CMMS, but you cannot install reliability.

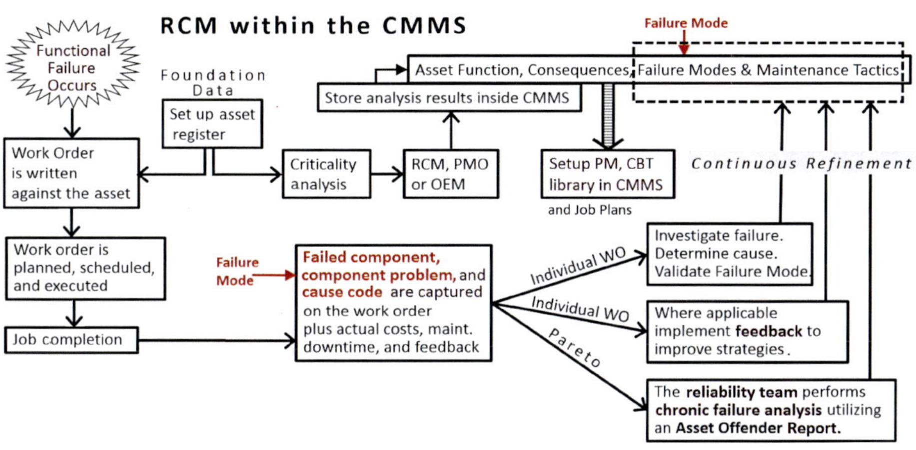

Figure F-1: This is the end-game.

Key Takeaways from this Book

- ✓ The failure mode should be captured directly on the Work Order record.
- ✓ The failure analytic should be designed early on because it will drive requirements for failure data, with involvement from the reliability engineer.
- ✓ Every organization would benefit from having a reliability team. They would drive failure analysis to optimize asset reliability and support operational excellence.
- ✓ This holistic solution places special emphasis on cause codes as 84% of all asset failures are tied to human factors.
- ✓ As an improvement initiative, chronic failure analysis provides the largest potential benefit (and ROI) within the CMMS platform and supports value-add decision making.

CHAPTER 1

Fundamentals Aren't Always Fundamental

Even among reliability professionals, there is sometimes confusion with definitions. For example, what exactly is asset management? In addition, key definitions can evolve over time as new concepts and technology are introduced. Most professionals agree, however, that asset reliability, work force productivity, and job safety are worthy objectives.

The Asset Management System

An organization's computerized maintenance management system (CMMS) alone does not make an asset management system. However, an asset management system cannot exist without a sound CMMS. The organization Reliabilityweb.com provides an asset management system design that ties together reliability engineering for maintenance, asset condition management, work execution management, leadership for reliability, and asset management strategies. This combination forms an asset management framework displayed as the Uptime Elements.

I believe a reliability program can also be defined as failure analysis, defect elimination, reliability centered maintenance (as RCM analysis), condition-based technology, and advanced work management processes (Figure 1-1). In both the framework and the program, we are talking about the interaction of software, process, and organization.

The process side starts with a vision/mission statement, goals and objectives by department, CMMS standard operating procedures, RACI charts (Responsible, Accountable, Consulted, and Informed), and business rules. The organizational side includes the executive sponsor, core team, business analyst, the reliability team, the system administrator (often IBM's Maximo), and power users (including planners and schedulers, the maintenance supervisor, and the warehouse coordinator).

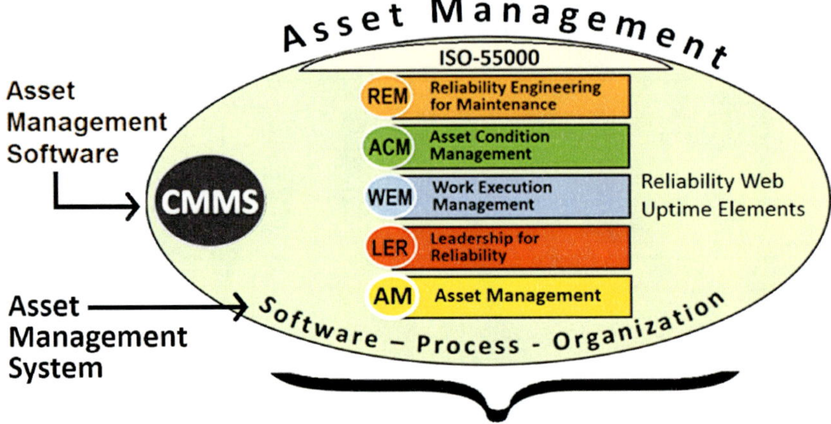

Figure 1-1: An asset management system.

The Asset Management System Should Vigorously Support Return on Asset

Asset reliability, maintainability, and work force productivity (as well as job safety) support operational excellence. Maintainability measures the ease of maintaining equipment, diagnosing problems, and restoring equipment to operation.

In Figure 1-2, we see that maintainability, work management, and reliability all contribute to the availability of the equipment. Reliability also contributes to performance and quality. Overall equipment effectiveness (OEE) is the product of maintainability, performance, and quality. It contributes to net profit margin, which is calculated by dividing net profit by total revenue. Return on assets (ROA) measures how efficient management is at using its assets to generate earnings, given that too many breakdowns and unplanned downtime impact reliability.

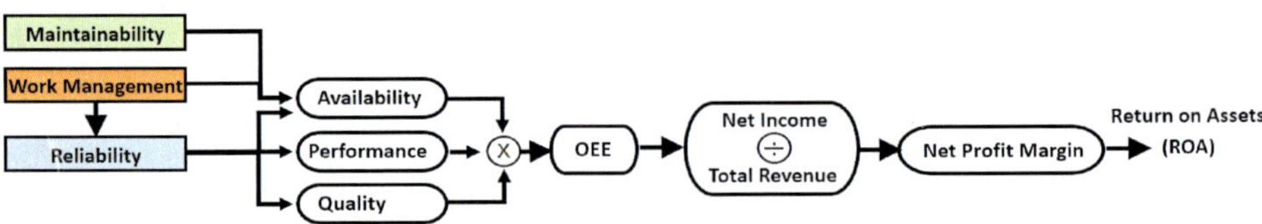

Figure 1-2: How well does a company operate its assets?

Conversely, a singular work management focus that ignores chronic failure analysis, root cause analysis, RCM analysis, defect elimination, and condition monitoring techniques will struggle to optimize ROA. For example, you can have 100% PM compliance on a weekly schedule, but be doing the wrong work. If you have never validated your PM/CBT library against RCM-suggested maintenance tactics, then you are potentially doing unnecessary work, introducing new defects, and increasing risk.

Reliability from a CMMS Perspective

A reliability program has many requirements. But I think that **chronic failure analysis** does not receive enough attention and has more potential return on investment than any other reliability initiative. Figure 1-3 further illustrates the interrelationship of software, process, and organization. Figure 1-4 connects the CMMS foundation data to precision maintenance followed by defect elimination. RCM analysis is then used to define the PM/CBT library. To close the loop, three techniques are used: work order feedback, chronic failure analysis, and root cause analysis.

Chronic failure analysis provides the bedrock of this design. Best-in-class design is the outcome from an interconnected strategy that starts with the asset, creates the ideal maintenance tactic, prioritizes work, captures feedback, and continually refines the PM/CBT library.

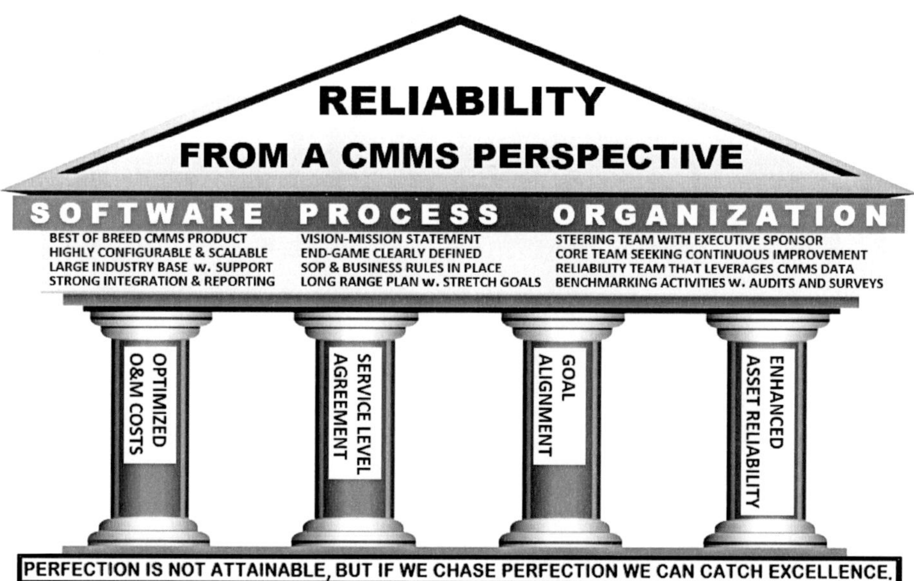

Figure 1-3: Reliability from a CMMS perspective.

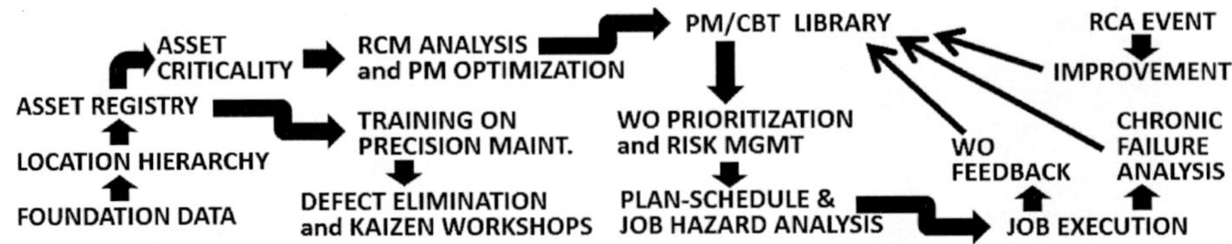

Figure 1-4: Closed loop process for continuous improvement.

Failure History Can Mean Different Things to Different People

If you asked maintenance technicians to explain failure history, they might say, "We record what we found, what we did, and the actual hours and material." In some cases, maintenance technicians provide suggestions about failure prevention. Unfortunately, any narrative text entries cannot be used to aggregate data or uniformly select and sort failure data. Proactive maintenance needs analytical tools that study history (e.g., repeat failures) to manage the future (Figure 1-5). Validated data are essential to managing by exception.

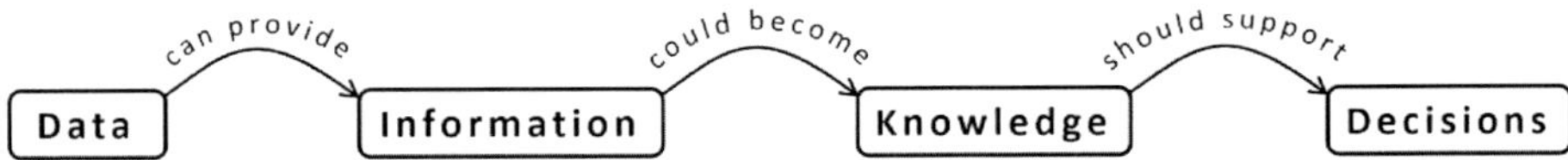

Figure 1-5: Data and decisions.

Table 1-1 looks at failure history in four different ways. How do we make failure history useful to all? Answer: By applying options 2, 3, and 4.

Table 1-1: Four Interpretations of Failure History

(1) No recorded history exists	In this unfortunate scenario, the staff primarily relies on person-to-person, verbal exchange (tribal knowledge). The person investigating an issue might talk directly with O&M staff to establish root cause. The CMMS is used primarily as a work order ticket system, which adds minimal predictive value in terms of failure history. *Note: This type of dialog is absolutely important but should augment, not replace CMMS data.*
(2) Search key word across many work orders.	I call this the "get lucky" approach whereby a specific word search is performed and, if it hits on any records, they are reviewed on screen, one work order at a time. Therefore, the organization relies on properly spelled words (in text fields) on each work order. The maintenance staff essentially owns this data because they put it in for this exact purpose. Consequently, they make every effort to record complete and accurate repair history. Unfortunately, this data cannot be aggregated.
(3) Pull up all work against one asset.	If the problem asset is known, that specific asset can be searched to find all history work orders. This technique helps the maintenance staff review prior work history. *Note: Most likely the failure event has already happened and the staff want to review history.*
(4) Perform structured failure analysis.	The CMMS failure data is used to help staff know where to focus, i.e., where are the worst offenders? For this approach to succeed, there must be validated failure data. Using a Pareto-style failure analytic, the organization can manage by exception and float the bad actors to the top of the list. From there, they select a specific asset and drill down through failure modes to failure causes. This entire process is called chronic failure analysis. It enables the leadership to become more proactive and optimize costs by analyzing recurring failures. *Note: In this scenario, the reliability team is performing Pareto analysis by grouping together the most frequently occurring events.*

Why Do Organizations Struggle with Failure Data (and Failure Analysis)?

The maintenance staff quite often view their primary role as "repair and replace" instead of "detect and prevent." As a result, when asked why (or how) an asset or component failed, they seldom know the specific causes of failure. Without a proper investigative process, there is a good chance that these failures will happen again. This type of reactive mode can lead to poor asset reliability.

10 Reasons Why CMMS Failure Data is Generally Lacking

All too often the CMMS contains poor failure data. This inadequacy impacts the organization in many ways. But to answer why CMMSs struggle, we must understand the various reasons:

1. A core team may not exist. This group is generally responsible for the overall operation and utilization of the CMMS. As a team, they would have functional-side representatives who understand the importance of creating a true knowledge base and the ability to leverage this data to make more informed decisions.
2. Sometimes there is no maintenance engineer, reliability engineer, or reliability champion at any level to perform investigative or root cause analysis.
3. Without a reliability engineer in place, the core team may not have designed or implemented the CMMS to support failure analysis. Such analysis requires a failure analytic and the necessary input fields for capturing failure data.
4. Sometimes there is no reliability team to run the failure analytic that identifies the worst offenders, drills down on failure modes, and reviews the data.
5. The CMMS products often do not have a decent failure analytic as part of the base product; nor can they perform a Pareto sort because the validated failure data does not exist.
6. Most CMMS products do not capture failure mode (failed component, component problem, and cause code) as part of their base product.
7. Most CMMS products only manage failure data at the asset level. They do not mention the component level (in validated fields).
8. There is a misunderstanding as to what exactly is a "cause" of failure. Many focus on the physical component and ignore the human factor aspect.
9. The failure analysis process as a whole may not be defined, documented, or performed.
10. The failure analysis process might exist solely as an informal sit-down meeting with department leads to discuss issues.

Key Concepts Defined

Pareto Sort

The term *Pareto sort* (or group sort) refers to different ways the failure data can be processed. A top-10 output needs to know the parameter on which to focus. The user answers a prompt as to how the report should group asset records. Examples include number of failures, MTBF, asset condition, maintenance downtime, age, and average annual maintenance cost divided by replacement cost (replacement asset value or RAV).

Different Types of Failure Analysis

Failure analysis can occur before a failure event and also after a failure event (Figure 1-6). RCM analysis (or PM optimization) identifies possible failure modes in anticipation of possible failures so that the appropriate maintenance tactic can be set up. In scenarios where a major event has occurred, a root cause analysis (RCA) is performed, usually specific to one asset or location. Chronic failure analysis, on the other hand, uses a Pareto sort to find the worst offenders (e.g., top 10).

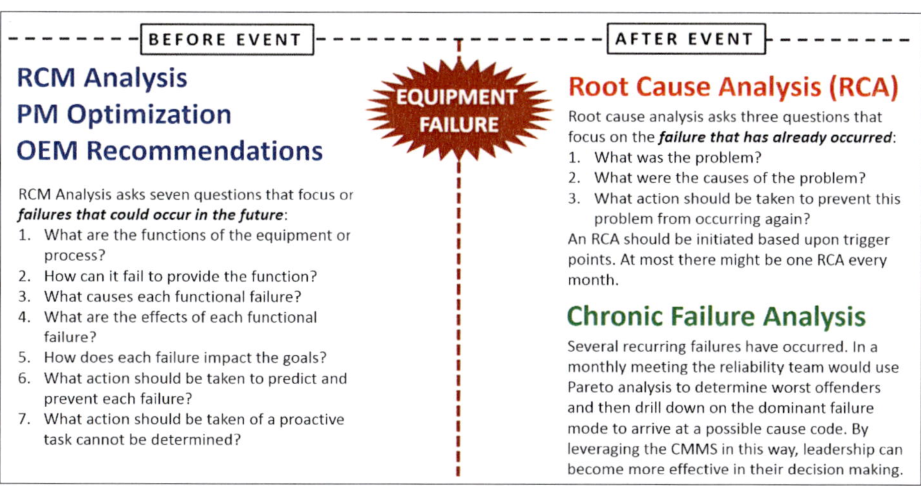

Figure 1-6: Failure analysis.

Chronic Failures

Chronic failures are recurring failures. They are not as significant or as costly as an RCA event. However, according to reliability leader Charles Latino, chronic failures of machines, systems, and people can occur daily in plants across the country. By eliminating these chronic failures, you could potentially reduce maintenance costs between 40% and 60%.

Chronic Failure Analysis

Chronic Failure Analysis is an advanced process for managing recurring failures. With the use of a Pareto-style failure analytic, the reliability team can identify bad actors. This enables them to manage by exception and begin identifying the root cause of their most significant issues. Chronic Failure Analysis depends on actionable failure data—specifically the failure mode—and a reliability team to dynamically drill down into the root cause.

If the language of RCM is failure mode, shouldn't the work order also capture a failure mode? This information would make it possible to perform direct comparisons inside the CMMS.

Chronic Failure Analysis Using the CMMS

Figure 1-7 discusses a better design that leverages the CMMS to perform chronic failure analysis. This design has several innovative elements:

- Capturing failure mode on the work order record
- Storing RCM analysis results directly inside the CMMS (which contains failure mode and maintenance tactics)
- Creating a Pareto-style failure analytic (asset offender report) with dynamic drill-down capability
- Role-wise, the reliability team running the failure analytic, drilling down, and making decisions

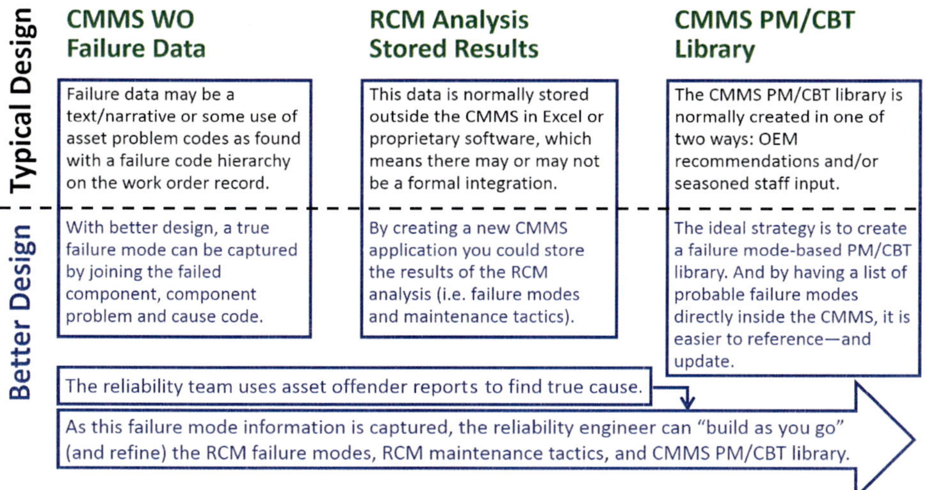

Figure 1-7: A unique design for chronic failure analysis.

Chronic Failure Analysis: Process and Data

Maintenance is performed primarily at the component level.

Best-in-class organizations successfully leverage failure data within the CMMS. Conversely, they do not rely on roundtable meetings with subjective analysis. If the CMMS needs to be configured, then so be it. The scenario illustrated in Figure 1-8 (parts a and b) starts with a functional failure.

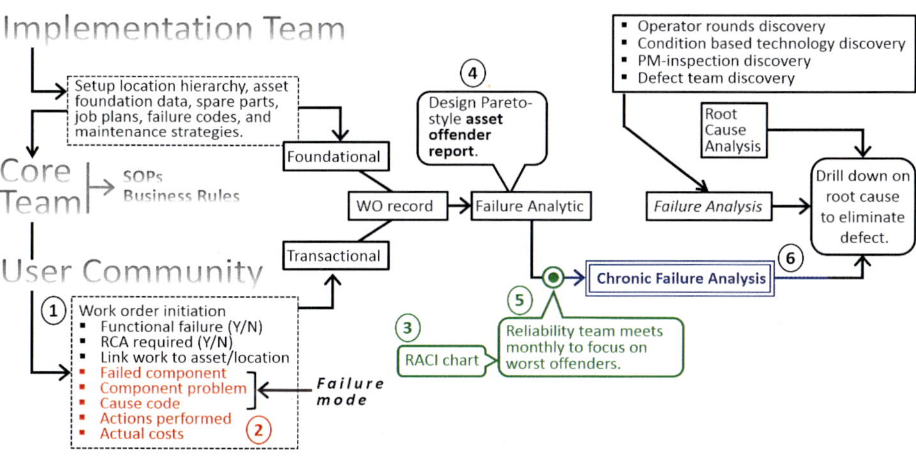

Figure 1-8a: Chronic Failure Analysis.

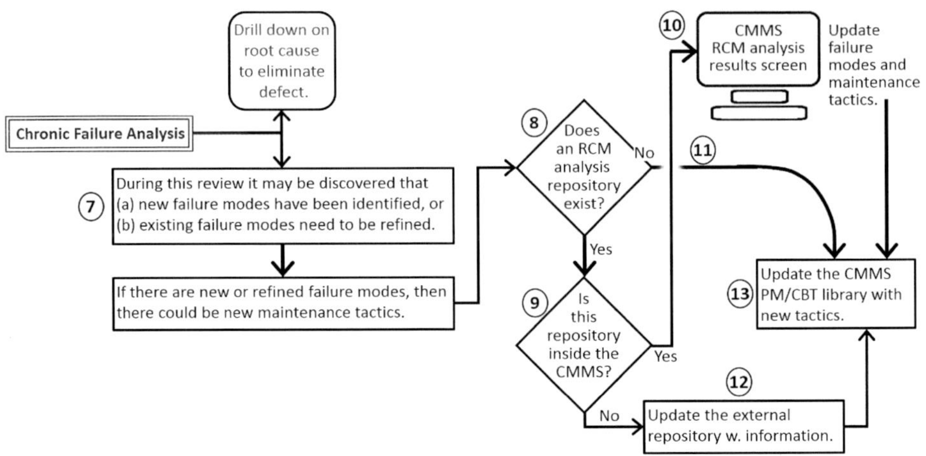

Figure 1-8b: New failure modes and tactics.

The design begins by collecting Work Order failure data (Steps 1, 2, and 3).

1. Work Order initiation. Document work required for a repair event. Link the Work Order to the location or asset and enter the problem description, problem code, and priority. Identify if this work involves a functional failure. Identify the work type, priority, and lead craft. Evaluate if RCA is required.
2. Job completion: Capture actual history (failure mode, actions performed, and actuals).
3. RACI chart. This document is created by the core team and identifies who does what in regards to updating the CMMS. Someone must be responsible for saying the work is done as well as updating the Work Order status (to complete). The RACI chart would also indicate who is allowed to insert/update foundation data. RACI stands for responsible, accountable, consulted, and informed.

There could be many functional failures over time. Those that are linked to the same asset and have similar problem codes can be called chronic failures. Chronic failure analysis is intended to identify those assets that have the most problems.

4. Pareto report. This is a failure analytic that in most cases needs to be designed and registered within the CMMS. It is normally best for the reliability team to design this report and then verify that the necessary inputs are being captured.
5. Reliability team meeting. In a monthly meeting, the reliability team leverages data in the CMMS by running the failure analytic to identify the problem assets and then drilling down on failure modes.

6. Chronic failure analysis. This is an advanced process that requires software/data, process/procedure, and roles/responsibilities to be interconnected. This process enables the reliability team to focus on bad actors and take corrective action.

The scenario illustrated in Figure 1-8b starts with discovery of new failure modes and/or maintenance tactics.

7. During the review process, new failure modes and maintenance tactics might be discovered. Their discovery may require update of the RCM analysis results and the CMMS PM/CBT library.
8. Not every organization has performed an RCM analysis (or PM optimization).
9. For those that did have an analysis performed, this data is stored in a repository of some type.
10. Having the repository reside directly inside the CMMS product makes it easier to link records together.
11. If no repository exists, the reliability team needs to still update the CMMS PM/CBT library.
12. If an external repository exists, then update this with new information.
13. The goal is reliability assurance. By updating the applicable RCM analysis repository and the CMMS PM/CBT library, we now have a living program that will help achieve higher ROA (return on asset) value.

Software-Process-Organization Make the System

An asset management system requires the interaction of software, process, and organization. Table 1-2 summarizes these key elements.

Table 1-2: The Significance of Software, Process, and Organization

Software / Data	Process / Procedure	Organization / Roles
• Design/build the asset offender report (failure analytic). • Store RCM analysis results inside the CMMS. • Place failure mode fields on work order screen as separate entities. • Add functional failure (Y/N). • Add RCA required (Y/N) • Set up automatic maintenance downtime capture. • Provide for asset condition capture during scheduled PM. • Allow for automatic routing and review of missing failed components. • Allow for formal work order feedback with routing and review.	• Document and train on the chronic failure analysis process. • Establish procedure to mandate asset condition during monthly PM. • Establish procedure to authorize ongoing refinement of RCM failure mode and maintenance tactics. • Establish process to capture at-risk assets. • Develop procedure to capture work order feedback and follow-up. • Develop procedure to implement defect elimination teams.	• Identify the reliability team. • Update the RACI chart as to who owns the failure mode library, who must provide failure mode data, and who must perform error checks.

Resultant Process Benefits

With this process, the reliability team (or reliability engineer) can continually refine maintenance tactics which, in turn, will optimize O&M costs. The team can always investigate a single breakdown or perform a root cause analysis on a single event. But the Pareto analysis (using the asset offender report) provides the best method for floating worst offenders to the top, and then drilling down on failure modes. The review team might also consider these questions:

1. Does this work order have the right failure mode entered?
2. Does the asset currently have the right maintenance strategy in place; does it address a specific failure mode?
3. If the answers to both questions are "Yes," then why did this failure occur?

Failure Data: Asset versus Component

CMMS manages the asset,
RCM manages the component.

Most CMMS products do an excellent job of identifying the asset record, failure class, and asset problem code. However, they do not do a good job of identifying the failed component, component problem, or cause code. There are multiple reasons for this: (a) CMMS product design, (b) lack of training relating to RCM concepts, and (c) poor setup of failure codes whereby they mix types such as components and human causes.

Figure 1-9 illustrates the challenge of discovering the root cause. You might ask: How does the asset problem code and asset cause code help the maintenance engineer with failure analysis? The answer is: It does not.

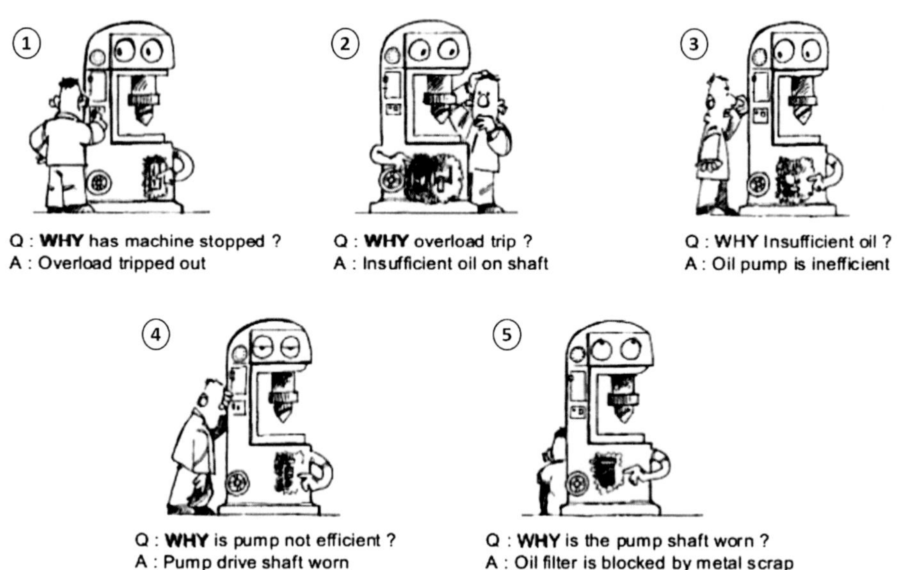

Figure 1-9: Identifying the cause. (*Image source: ABB)*

Recognizing the Failure Mode

Maintenance is performed at the component level. When an asset is returned to service after a corrective maintenance activity, there is usually a failed component which was replaced (or possibly repaired). This failed component is the first element of the failure mode. Until you speak the language of RCM, i.e., failure mode, you will systematically struggle to determine root cause.

The CMMS products often just ask for the affected asset and problem code for the asset. If the asset is a drill press and it has stopped, the problem code might be "Stopped." But why has it stopped? By asking the "5 Whys," a methodology for cause analysis, the investigator can usually arrive at the root cause. Figure 1-9, circle 5, shows the oil filter to be blocked with metal scrap. Thus the failed component is the "oil filter," the component problem is "blocked," and the cause is "operator did not clean filter at start of shift."

Figure 1-10 comes from RCM facilitator Douglas Plucknette. It shows a three-part failure mode. The tan box shows a typical CMMS design that focuses on the asset. Circles 1, 2, and 3 represent the failure mode. Most reliability engineers require all three parts (component, component problem, and cause code) to properly identify the maintenance tactic.

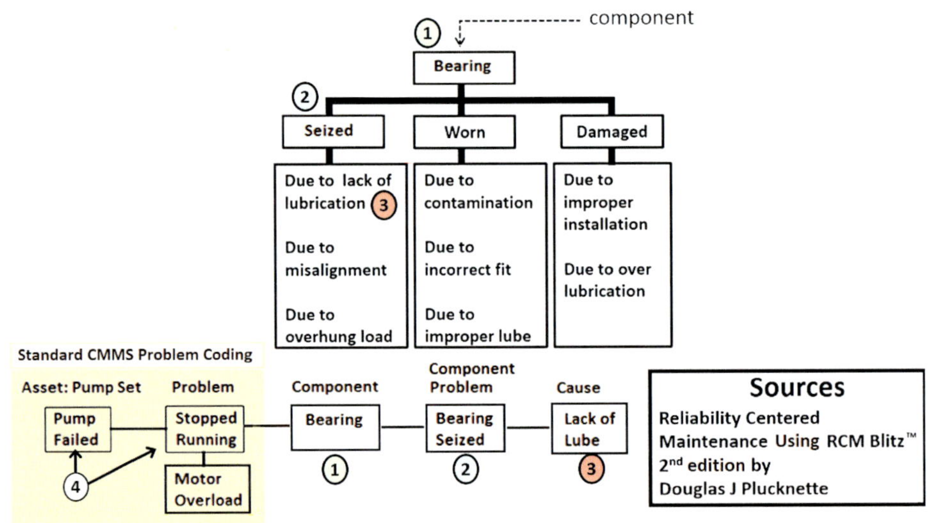

Figure 1-10: Three-part failure mode.

RCM Standard Frequently Refers to Failure Mode

By conducting a word search within the technical standard SAE JA1011, the term failure mode appears several times (in yellow) just on one page (Figure 1-11). Furthermore, the RCM analysis process requires the failure mode to determine the corresponding maintenance tactics. Therein, the failure mode is critical to reliability centered maintenance.

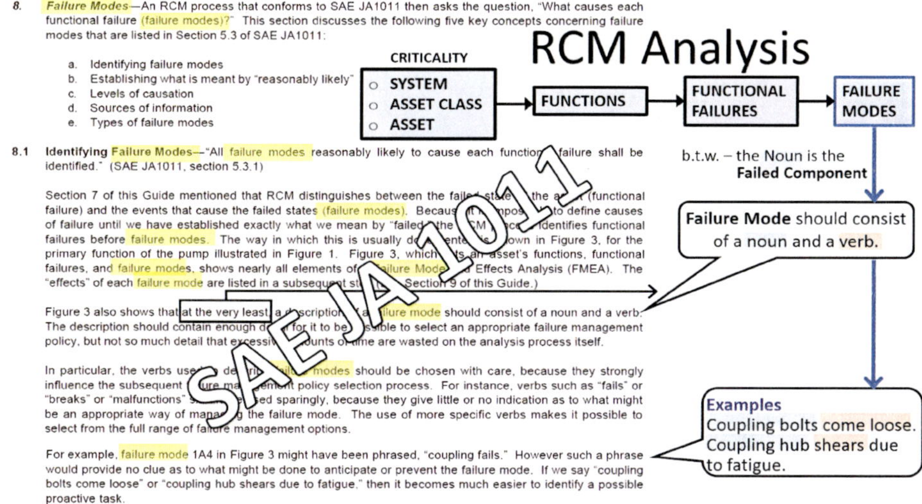

Figure 1-11: Failure mode as used within the RCM Standard.

Three-Way Match

With proper configuration of the CMMS, the reliability team can establish a three-way match of the Work Order, the PM/CBT, and the RCM analysis (Figure 1-12). This approach supports continuous improvement of the maintenance strategies within the RCM analysis repository and the CMMS PM/CBT library.

Circle 1 identifies the application for storing the time and usage-based maintenance strategies. There is a best practice which says every maintenance strategy should be linked back to a failure mode. Circle 2 identifies the typical work order entry screen. What is not typical, though, is that this screen captures a true failure mode. Most CMMS products out of the box do not. Circle 3 identifies a new application within the CMMS product called RCM Analysis. This screen and table store the results of any analysis. It can also serve as a build-as-you-go repository for updates as new information is discovered.

Without these connections, it is difficult or highly unlikely for the user community (e.g., reliability team, maintenance staff, planners) to make refinements to existing maintenance strategies.

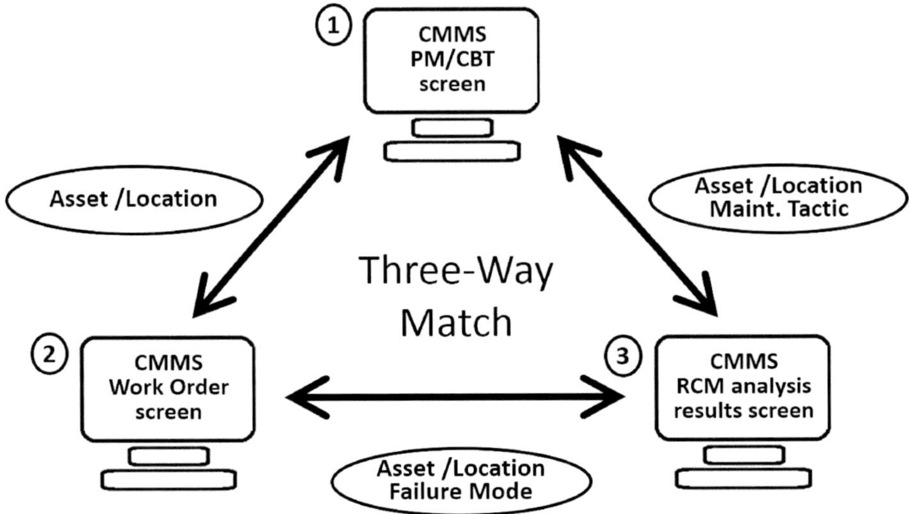

Figure 1-12: Three-way match.

Why Focus on Work Order Failure Modes?

The standards for reliability centered maintenance refer to failure mode in every capacity. Shouldn't the CMMS have the same terminology and emphasis? If RCM analysis produces an output that determines the likely failure modes and suggested maintenance tactics, wouldn't it make sense to also capture the failure mode on the work order for purposes of comparison? Further, if the Work Order failure mode has the same choice lists as the RCM analysis review, then data synchronization becomes even easier. And once the failure modes are in synch, you can focus on maintenance strategies, which is the real end game.

Reliability engineers now have the ability to refine as you go a comprehensive library of failure modes and tactics. For the first time, they have actionable data in one system to help the organization make more informed decisions. They might begin by asking a series of thought-provoking questions:

- Why did this failure mode occur if we already had this failure mode documented in the RCM analysis?
- Was the suggested maintenance tactic incorrect? Were the failure modes incorrect?
- If the RCM analysis is missing this Work Order failure mode, should we add it?

No matter how good the RCM facilitator may be, there will never be a perfect analysis. Therefore, the asset management system should be designed to support a living program that encourages continuous refinement.

Failure mode capture on the Work Order may not reveal the absolute root cause, but it is certainly more informative than problem codes at the asset level.

CHAPTER 2

Precision Maintenance Needs Precision Data

Precision maintenance is a term not widely known, but it is certainly performed every day by maintenance trades. Proper installation of equipment involves fasteners, alignment, balancing, and lubrication. Attention to detail helps staff and machines deliver longer-lasting reliable service. On the other hand, recurring equipment problems are often due to a lack of precision maintenance skills.

Understanding the Data

Structured and Unstructured

Structured data consists of master data, planning data, transactional data, and operational data (Figure 2-1).

Another term for master data is foundation data. This includes asset registry, location hierarchy, and item master. Within the asset record, for example, there are several fields which further qualify the asset, such as classification, manufacturer, installation date, and failure class. When the user links an asset to a Work Order, the failure class automatically crosses over to the Work Order. Transactional data is very important in that it ties the actual costs, failure codes, and log notes to a date.

Unstructured data consists of free format narrative text, reference links, paper-based data, and even tribal knowledge.

Both types of data—structured and unstructured—are important on the Work Order. By definition, all forms of structured data are validated, meaning the value is chosen either from a table of records or a choice list. This means that structured data will never be misspelled. Furthermore, only structured data can be aggregated to perform Pareto-style analysis.

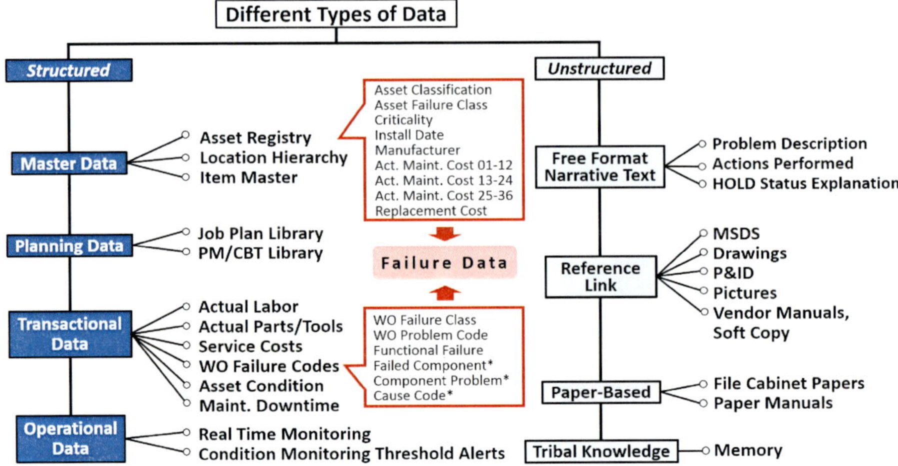

Figure 2-1: Different data types.

In the life of a Work Order, different roles perform updates. For example, the requestor initially describes the problem with a narrative; the planner/scheduler plans and schedules the work; and at job completion, the tradesperson enters actuals and completes the failure data—including actions performed. Additional roles can be used to complete the failure mode. For example, the failed component would be known by the tradesperson. The component problem code might be entered by the maintenance supervisor. In addition, the cause code might be determined by the maintenance engineer. Narrative text is still important and can be word searched, but it is not useful for aggregating data.

One of the historical problems with paper-based systems (paper copies are stored in file cabinets) is the person doing the filing has to make a choice. Do we file this paper by Work Order number, report date, asset identifier, or something else? Once that decision is made, you just can't re-sort the information the way you could on a computer.

From a failure analysis standpoint, we are most interested in actionable data. The combination of asset registry data and Work Order failure codes gives us structured failure data. It is this data which can be aggregated, sorting worst offenders (assets/locations) to the top for selection, and subsequent drilldown on failure modes to arrive at true cause.

Caution: Too many organizations overlook key fields on the asset record (meaning they fail to populate these fields). Examples include criticality, replacement cost, installation date (age), asset classification, failure class, and manufacturer. These fields are critical in the failure analytic. Some are used in the Pareto sort and some are used for filtering.

Figure 2-2 takes the advice of writer Stephen Covey, which is to design with the end in mind.

Capturing the right data is not easy. So many things can go wrong. Failure analysis, being an advanced process, has three perspectives: software/data, process/procedure, and roles/responsibilities. What is the right data? Exactly what data should be collected? The answer to these questions is to design the CMMS with decision making in mind. The failure analytic tells us what fields to capture and processes to implement.

Step 1 The reliability team (or core team) should design the failure analytic on paper. This report is intended to support chronic failure analysis by extracting a Pareto-style output. The report itself is a two-step process whereby the users select the worst offender (possibly one from each group-sort) and then drill down on the failure mode.

Step 2 Working backwards, the users are given choices as to what group-sort option to use. It may be that they run the report multiple times, for each group-sort.

2a Considering that there is a lot of routine maintenance, we are really only after those Work Orders with a functional failure. With that information, we can then identify the asset with the most failures or go after the mean time between failure (MTBF). Alternatively, you could go choose mean time to repair (MTTR) instead of MTBF.

2b Although the CMMS may have the capability of capturing downtime, it is up to the users to enter this data in the right fields. But if the total click-count is too high, users will sometimes avoid entering this information. If that happens, and this failure data is essential to the report, the system administrators should investigate a method to make data capture easier.

2c For the CMMS you are using, there may not be a documented method for capturing asset condition. But again, seeing how this data point would be quite useful to trend over time, the reliability team (or core team) should draw up a process that captures the asset condition during a scheduled PM/CBT activity.

2d One of the most powerful metrics for identifying bad actors is the average annual maintenance cost divided by replacement cost for a given asset. Because this type of calculation could be time consuming to process, it is best to set up three historical fields on the asset record and then automatically fill these in once a week via an automation script which executes on a regular schedule (called cron task). Also note, it is important for the replacement cost to be entered as well.

2e Another useful parameter is the asset age. Some assets are under a capital renewal plan. You need to know when it was installed or overhauled.

2f Using all this information, you can multiply the asset condition by the criticality and gain another perspective on which assets to set your focus.

Step 3 These are the prerequisites. The software could be perfectly designed, but if the working level is not entering the data, then all is lost. Also, if the click-count is too high, the system administrator needs to figure out a way to make this process simpler. Other prerequisites include clear roles, documented processes, and end-user training. During this training event, it is important to explain how this data helps the organization find defects and become more proactive, thereby optimizing production and reducing maintenance costs.

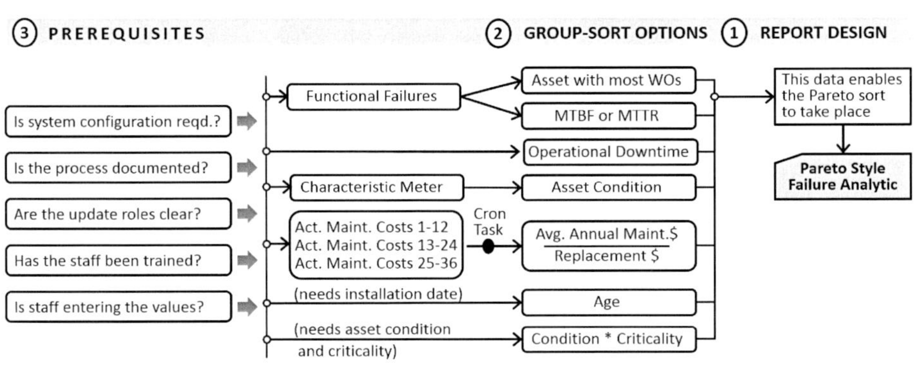

Figure 2-2: Linking Outputs to Inputs.

Asset Management Needs a Reliability Champion

The CMMS software is just one piece of an asset management system. Many implementations are software projects whereby stakeholders focus on product configuration, data loads, and training (Figure 2-3). Although functional users may be members of the team, they seldom have adequate knowledge to design a Pareto-style failure analytic with dynamic drill-down capability. You cannot assume the CMMS will have a failure analytic that meets your needs.

Many organizations today have either a reliability champion, a reliability engineer, or a reliability team—but they are not part of the CMMS implementation or operating teams. The CMMS administration would be well served to involve this staff. Reliability engineers could design a failure analytic to leverage failure data within the CMMS. Plus they would have a good understanding of failure mode. A reliability team would be involved with chronic failure analysis. A reliability champion would be familiar with asset criticality, root cause analysis, RCM analysis, condition based technologies, and defect elimination.

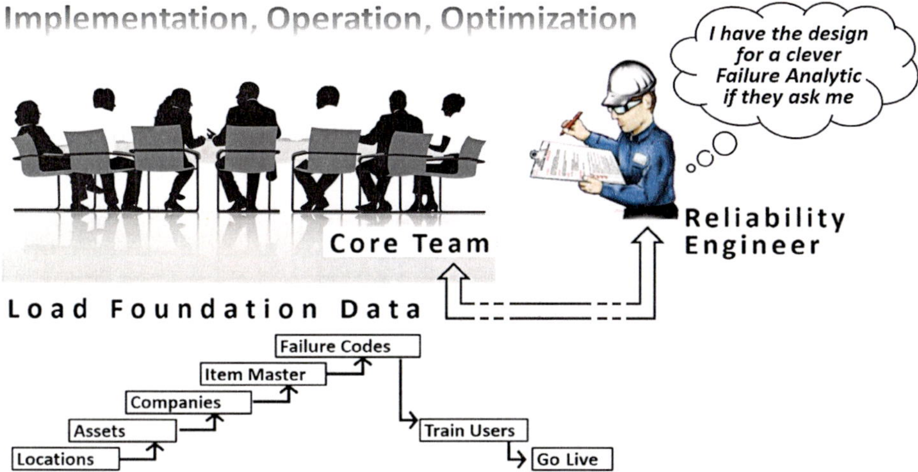

Figure 2-3: Implementation, Operation, and Optimization.

Individual Fields Provide Plenty of Combinations

There are different thoughts on how best to capture a failure mode. Options include (1) enter free-format text, (2) acquire a prebuilt set of failure modes, or (3) use an interconnection of key fields. I prefer this last approach. By using three separate fields on the Work Order screen, you can capture the failed component, component problem, and cause code. This approach provides many more potential combinations for you to choose from than a prebuilt list would provide—with less clicking. Lastly, by breaking the failure mode into three distinct pieces, each with its own domain (choice list), the designers have greater ease to manage changes.

A validated field is one that has a list of choices. The user must select from this set of values. This approach eliminates any spelling errors and helps the user find the right answer. Validated fields are also called actionable fields in that their values can be selected, sorted, and aggregated using SQL commands, whereas free-format text cannot. (SQL is structured query language; it selects, updates, or deletes records in a database.)

An asset or asset class is made up of components. If we assume there are 50 possible components, of which each of these might have 18 component problem codes, and each of the problem codes could have 13 possible causes, then the grand total would be 11,700 combinations. Imagine having to choose from a single large list with that many choices.

Figure 2-4 shows a large total possible combinations with the simple use of three separate fields. If each field had a set of choices, such as 50, 18 and 13 then the total combinations would be 11,700. Separate fields are also easier to update.

Possible failure mode combinations	=	Failed Components	X	Component Problems	X	Cause Code
	=	50	X	18	X	13
	=	11,700 possible combinations				

Figure 2-4: Failure mode combinations.

Utilization of a Failure Code Hierarchy (FCH)

Some CMMS products have a failure code hierarchy for storing failure codes. Before explaining this concept, let's review the different types of Work Order failure codes. The Work Order can have a failure class and an asset problem code. According to the RCM standard, we *should* have a failed component, component problem, and cause code (which is called a failure mode). Historically, CMMS products did not accommodate for the failure mode.

On the surface, a failure code hierarchy appears to be a technically advanced design for showing only those failure codes that apply to the higher level category. The typical design has failure class, problem code, cause code, and remedy.

If either of these include a component (from the equipment), then I can see how the values could be different. But let's assume there is no component in this hierarchy design. If that is the case, then we should develop an identical set of problem codes, cause codes, and remedy codes. This negates the need for a hierarchical design that increase the number of clicks for the user and becomes unnecessarily cumbersome to maintain.

Let's continue with the hierarchy discussion. The standard failure code hierarchy (FCH) has four levels, which I call Level 1, Level 2, Level 3, and Level 4. If users introduce components into the FCH, the components will interfere with capturing (human factor-related) cause codes. Over time, you get a mishmash of codes (problems, components, and causes) all in the same level. Quite often, the front line staff are so overwhelmed with the amount of clicking and the size of the lists that they just give up—and enter nothing.

There are other problems with the FCH design. For one, it can become quite onerous and unwieldy. Utilization of a FCH usually requires a higher click count to enter failure codes. Also, since an FCH is essentially a prebuilt failure list, some RCM practitioners believe it is not practical to ever come up with a comprehensive list. Lastly, failure coding is not a one-and-done process. As problems evolve in the plant, it is highly likely that more details will be needed to expand upon an engineering issue. Refinement should be expected—and should be easily performed.

In the end, all you need is the asset failure class and problem code along with the failed component and component problem. Overall, this failure data needs to be easy to maintain (i.e., add new values) and not overwhelm the maintenance trades. When missing values are discovered, an easy feedback mechanism should be provided for the worker to enter and the reviewer to approve.

The ideal use of a failure code hierarchy is to use Level 1 for the asset failure class and Level 2 for the asset problem code. Beyond that, the failure mode is best stored as three separate fields.

Mixing asset failure codes with component codes together tends to confuse the user and make reporting difficult. Figure 2-5 shows three design options that users sometimes choose to implement. Unfortunately they all have bad results.

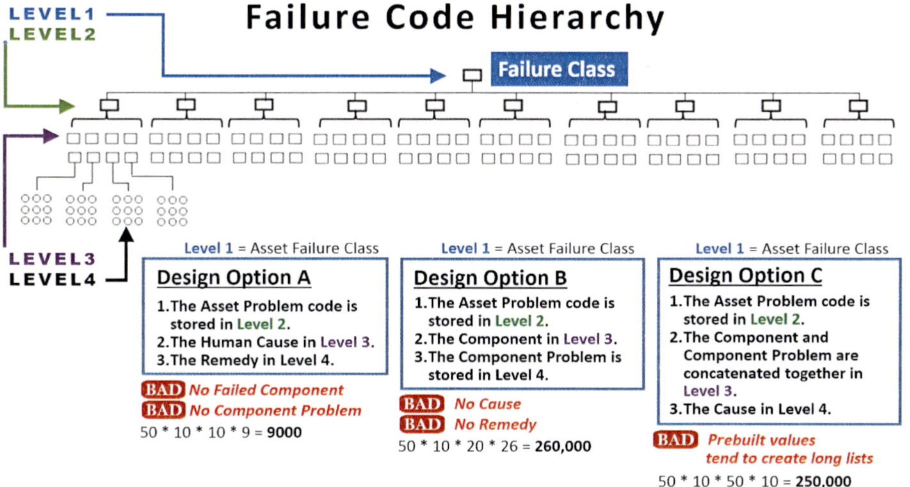

Figure 2-5: Failure code hierarchy (FCH).

Other considerations regarding the FCH design:

- If one assumed there were 25–30 standard problem codes, wouldn't it be better to just place them in a standalone field so you wouldn't have to maintain this same list in multiple places?

- If one assumed there were 10–12 standard remedy codes, wouldn't it be better to also place them in a standalone field?
- According to manufacturing consultant Winston Ledet, 84% of equipment failures are due to human influence. If this is true, any failure code design should accommodate for capturing human factors.
- Because failure mode capture can be quite involved, it is helpful to set up a stepped review process using pie charts as done with the failure analytic. This will be shown in Chapter 4.

What Is Failure History?

Failure History for the Maintenance Staff

If you ask the maintenance staff for their definition of failure history, they might say, "We need it to show us previous work performed as to the reported problem, the actions performed, and the materials used." They would probably add that they want as much narrative as possible about what was done, using text fields. Then when they have an asset failure, they can simply search on that same asset number to find all previous work, at which point, they can view these records on line or print out the Work Orders. Collectively this information helps the maintenance staff perform their current job. In other words, *the equipment* is in charge.

Failure History per the Reliability Engineer

Depending on how the organization is established, there may be a reliability champion, a reliability engineer, or even a reliability team. With this role, we might also assume there is a department goal to reduce reactive maintenance and optimize O&M costs. To achieve that goal, the department would leverage the CMMS to its fullest extent to identify worst offenders and defective elimination plans. In order to do this, the department must be able to aggregate data from the failure history in order to perform chronic failure analysis. If successful, they can manage by exception and make more informed decisions—whereby *they* are in charge.

There Are Several Forms of Failure Analysis

According to reliability expert and consultant Jack Nicholas, Pareto analysis can also be a trigger for RCM analysis. The Pareto can tell you what is causing your organization the most pain. By evaluating the top 20% to 30% of the results, you can then identify which systems or areas to further analyze.

There is also root cause analysis (RCA), which focuses on a specific asset that experienced a major event. RCA can be separated into three cases:

- Case 1: Performed by the operators on the line to address minor production issues
- Case 2: Performed by maintenance and operations to address minor failures
- Case 3: Performed by maintenance, operations, engineering, and management to address significant failures

An example of a Case 1 RCA process is the "five whys." This process involves asking the same question five or more times to arrive at the root cause. These little RCAs are completed in the moment by those involved.

The Significance of Proper Investigation

The purpose of failure analysis is to find out why something failed. The investigation phase is also called creative disassembly. There is a small window of opportunity to gather this evidence; maintenance staff should be careful to not throw away evidence. Creative disassembly makes us gather all data that could identify the causes of premature failure.

There might be a business rule saying, if a Work Order is marked as functional failure and the work is for a high priority asset, a cross-functional team must begin immediate investigation. This team would also look at equipment performance standards, the prescribed maintenance strategies, past PM/CBT activity, and Work Order failure data, and also talk with everyone involved (including operations, maintenance, and engineering).

Creative disassembly is an important part of precision maintenance. This analysis is necessary to avoid recurrence and prevent future failures for the same cause. The review process may be conducted by one person or may depend on the severity of the failure along with criticality of the asset. Without proper creative disassembly, there is a good chance the real cause will be missed and the defect will happen again, even after installing a brand new asset.

Failure Mode Is Essential to Failure Analysis

If the intent is to leverage the CMMS for failure history, the failure mode must exist on the Work Order as validated data. The failure mode is a combination of failed component, component problem, and cause code. Being the language of RCM, it provides the ability to dive down through the component problem to a possible cause. The failure mode also provides a way to compare a reported problem to the RCM analysis results—which stores failure modes along with suggested maintenance strategies. The reliability team may ask why this failure occurred (for the given asset) if it was already analyzed. Or, it may be discovered that the RCM analysis never mentioned this particular failure mode. Again, since the failure mode provides a common language, this process facilitates ready comparison that otherwise may not happen.

Asset Failure History versus Component Failure History

Many CMMS products track failure history at the asset level. This has been the norm for a very long time. The work order is linked to an asset number that has an asset description, asset classification, and failure class. This asset information crosses over to the work order. The users then enter the problem code for the asset. For example, the asset may be stopped. Unfortunately, this is seldom enough detail for reliability engineers as they cannot determine the failure mode direct from the CMMS. They may, however, capture this detail by gleaning the narrative fields or by talking with the O&M technicians, all of which takes additional time.

All equipment has components. Components are those items that are essential to operability but have no autonomous function by themselves. In the process of repair maintenance, it is the component that typically gets repaired or replaced. It is highly likely that the failed component will be known at the time of the repair so that the CMMS can be updated at job completion. The key question is, "Will this component be identified in a text field or a validated field?"

Failure Data Interaction with the Asset Offender Report

Table 2-1 describes the different types of failure data as used by the asset offender report.

The Asset Offender Report (AOR) makes use of failure data three ways: filtering, group sorts, and dynamic drilldown. With the help of report prompts, the user can filter records based on a selection, for example, those records where the asset priority equals 1. These prompts also ask the user to specify a group sort field, such as downtime. Once the Pareto analysis is performed, the bad actors float to the top of the list. The user can then select one of those assets to drill down on the failure modes.

Because most CMMS products rely on a relational database, the makeup of this database includes tables, rows, and columns (also called fields). A given row can have many columns of which one might be the primary key. It is called a relational database because the tables can have many joint relationships. When referencing a field, therefore, you must specify the table name and the field name. This information is shown in Column 4 of Table 2-1.

Table 2-1: Types of Failure Data as Used by the Asset Offender Report

Field Title	How Used	Example	Table Field Name
Asset	Asset primary key	Feedwater Pump	
Functional Failure	This is a Yes-No field to indicate that asset degradation is below the minimal accepted performance level. A value of Yes would drive the MTBF and MTTR calculations.	Entered as Yes or No	Workorder.newFuncFail
Asset Failure Class	Assets as a group may fall under the same failure class, meaning they have similar problem codes.	Pumps, Valves, Autoclaves, Heat Exchangers	Workorder.failurecode
Asset Problem	Problem Code for the asset. This field, if populated, drives the MTBF calculation.	Stopped	Workorder.problemcode
Component	Failed component. This is part 1 of 3 for the failure mode. The list of failed components would be determined by the failure class.	Bearing, Impeller, Seal, Piping, Coupling	Workorder.newFailComponent
Component Problem	Component problem code. This is part 2 of 3 for the failure mode.	Seized	Workorder.newCompProblem
Component Cause	This is part 3 of 3 for the failure mode and represents the final cause code. This field is automatically populated by either the Tactical, Human Factor, or Workmanship fields.	The users work their way through Tactical (Cause 1), Human Factor (Cause 2), and Workmanship (Cause 3) fields, but can stop at any one of the three. This stopping point becomes the final cause.	Workorder.newFinalCause

Table 2-1 Continued

Field Title	How Used	Example	Table Field Name
Tactical Cause Code (Cause 1)	This is the highest level of cause codes. The Tactical Cause is entered by the maintenance technician. The value "Human Factor" is chosen only when the other choices do not apply—in which case Cause 2 is required.	Force Majeure, Normal Wear, Aging, Power Failure, Human Factor	Workorder.newTacticalCause
Human Factor Code (Cause 2)	This is the second of three possible cause codes; entered by the maintenance supervisor. The value "Workmanship" is only chosen when the other choices do not apply—in which case Cause 3 is required.	Storage-Handling Vendor Setup Test Design Flaw Mgmt Oversight Defective Parts O&M Procedure Bad Poor Housekeeping Operating the Asset Improper PM Cycle Wrong Maint Strategy PM/CBT Skipped Workmanship	Workorder.newFactorCause

Table 2-1 Continued

Field Title	How Used	Example	Table Field Name
Workmanship Code (Casue3)	This is the third of three possible cause codes; entered by the maintenance/ reliability engineer. Any value entered here becomes the final cause. *Note: If leadership desires to permanently eliminate this defect, they should consider populating Human Oversight.*	Moisture Over Temperature Power Supply Stability Assembly Error Improper Tension Improper Mounting Misalignment Out Of Balance Incorrect Fastening Induced Vibration Component Distortion Lube Failure Contamination	Workorder.newWorkCause
Human Oversight	This type of dialogue might be done only on critical equipment and significant recurring failures that have a systemic or latent cause. This value is entered by the maintenance manager after a one-on-one discussion with the staff member.	Skills Deficiency Lack of Motivation Scope-to-Skill Mismatch No Repair Procedure Procedure Inaccurate No Training for this Procedure No Value Seen in Precision Maint.	Workorder.newLatentCause *Note:* This field might be visible only to the maintenance manager.

Table 2-1 Continued

Field Title	How Used	Example	Table Field Name
Remedy	These are generic actions performed	Adjust/Align/Tune/Reset/Tighten Calibrate Clean/Dry-out/Polish Inspect Lubricate Modify/Alter/Reconfigure/Resize Overhaul/Rebuild Correct Fluid Levels Repack Repair Replace With New Component Recharge Thaw Out Train User	Workorder.newRemedy

Table 2-1 Continued

Field Title	How Used	Example	Table Field Name
Asset Condition	This is a subjective value entered by the maintenance technician or inspector while performing a scheduled PM/ CBT. It is another way to monitor and trend the entire asset portfolio and take proactive action. This is a group-sort option on the asset offender report.	**1-Normal state:** There is little or no degradation in performance). **2-Warning state:** There is some degradation in performance but perhaps insufficient to warrant an intervention. **3-Alarm state**: There is sufficient degradation in performance to warrant an intervention either immediately OR at the next available downturn. **4-Critical state**: There is significant degradation in performance to warrant an immediate intervention.	This value is stored as a transactional record under a characteristic meter for a given asset.
Asset Downtime	Refers to operational downtime. This is a group-sort option on the asset offender report.	Total downtime hours for the asset.	

Field Title	How Used	Example	Table Field Name
Asset Performance Metric (as a percentage)	This metric provides a normalized value to fairly rank all assets as to performance condition. This is a group-sort option on the asset offender report.	(Average annual maintenance cost / replacement cost) * 100	This is dynamically calculated by the Asset Offender Report at run time.
Install Date	Provides asset age. This is a group-sort option on the asset offender report.	Entered or not entered.	Asset.installdate
At Risk	A given asset is bookmarked by O&M Manager that is having engineering issues. This information is displayed in margin of asset offender report.	Flagged or not flagged.	This information is stored using a bookmark against the given asset.
Asset Warranty	A given asset can have a warranty expiry date. This information is displayed in margin of asset offender report.	Entered or not. If entered it may be active or not.	Asset.expirydate
Actual maintenance costs as stored on asset record	These costs are stored on the asset record, and updated weekly via a cron task using an automation script. The performance metric reads these three values when calculating the average annual maintenance cost.	On the asset main screen, you can add three fields to store actual costs: 1–12 months, 13–24 months, and 25–36 months	asset.newMonths1to12 asset.newMonths13to24 asset.newMonths25to36

Field Title	How Used	Example	Table Field Name
Asset Criticality	This field indicates asset importance. This information can be used as a filter for the asset offender report.	Entered or not entered.	Asset.priority
Asset Class	This field groups together like assets by function.	Classification records are created and then linked to an asset as a specification template.	Normally it is the top level which is used for filtering.
Asset Manufacturer	This is the company/ vendor who made the asset. This field can be used for filtering.	Entered or not entered.	Asset.manufacturer
Failure Mode	The failure mode consists of the failed component, component problem and cause code. The failure mode is used by the asset offender report to dynamically drill down for the selected asset to arrive at a root cause.	Theoretically, every functional failure should have a failure mode identified.	The failure mode is dynamically created by joining the following fields from the Workorder table: newFailComponent newCompProblem newFinalCause

Understanding Failure Mode Significance

The failure mode provides the common link from the Work Order to the RCM/PMO analysis results to the PM/CBT library. Because maintenance is performed at the component level, it is important to capture failure data at this level.

Chronic Failure Analysis Needs the Failure Mode

Most asset intensive industries have a CMMS product. Some organizations understand how to manage by exception. Proactive organizations focus on worst offenders and manage their time accordingly. Chronic failure analysis, as an advanced process, has five crucial steps (Figure 2-6).

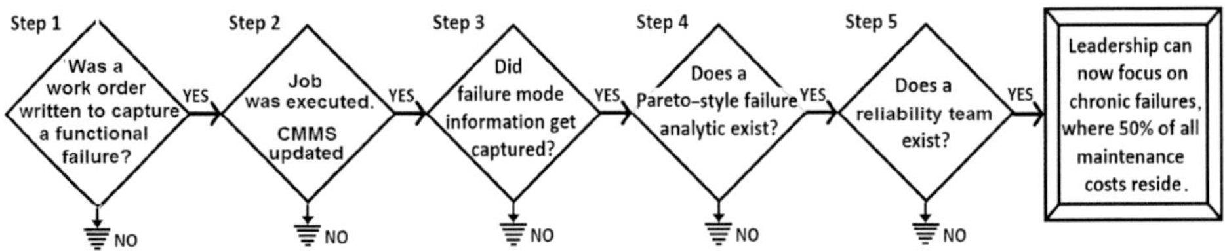

Figure 2-6: Prerequisites to chronic failure analysis.

The first step is to identify repair work that has a functional failure.

The assumption is that the maintenance staff perform proper updates to the CMMS.

This step assumes maintenance staff enter the correct failed component, component problem, and cause code at job completion.

The reliability team should design a failure analytic that meets their needs. This report would identify bad actors and permit dynamic drilldown on failure modes.

Best-in-class organizations will have a reliability team. In a monthly setting, this group will leverage failure data using a failure analytic to make more informed decisions on maintenance strategy, skilled trades training, and defect elimination.

Caution: If a reliability team (or similar) is not in place, then there is no one to give the report to. This greatly undermines the process and minimizes benefit.

The Failure Mode Is Linked to an Asset

The work order is usually tied to an asset (or location). The selected asset will have a failure class and problem code linked to the work order. This asset accumulates costs, downtime, and meter values. PM activities may be tied to the asset. Spare parts are also linked to the asset. Once the repair job is complete, the maintenance technician can identify the failure mode. At this point we have linked the failure mode to the asset.

Possible Criteria for Determining an Asset

The following list names the criteria a company might use to determine if a component is an actual asset or just a component. Every organization will have its own set of criteria. The important point is that you have one.

1. Equipment and tools that have replacement value over $5,000; cost to repair/replace is high
2. Equipment that would benefit from a diagnostic work history
3. Equipment that requires scheduled maintenance (or testing); has PM/CBT

schedule attached (or run-hours based)

4. Equipment that requires spare parts be maintained in stock
5. Equipment that would benefit from periodic financial replacement analysis
6. Equipment monitored by the SCADA system
7. Need to track downtime
8. Has internal or external regulations that address this specific asset
9. Safety-related
10. Automation equipment represented on piping and instrument diagrams
11. Occasionally moved from location to another location; swapped out
12. Assets that frequently get repaired and could be modified (altered in design)
13. Need total life cycle cost tracked; assets may be sent off-site to repair vendors (need to capture these costs too)
14. Has there been past significant failure history
15. Need to identify failure trending on this entity; and perform failure analysis
16. Asset needs to have specification data defined
17. Asset needs to have meter data
18. Asset has warranty information, if entered, the work order will auto-generate warning
19. Asset may or may not be serialized; not all serialized components are assets
20. Asset may or may not be tagged
21. Assets should have an installation date, criticality, spare parts, replacement cost, manufacturer, cost to-date based on actuals, and a maintenance strategy
22. A "system impact" to production/operations if asset is not running
23. Requirement for formal feedback including asset condition
24. Signature sign-offs are procedurally required
25. Requirement for keeping paper history for determined time period; regulatory requirements

Identifying the Component

It is important to not confuse an asset with a component or a part. A component can be a stocked part, but not all parts are components. The asset bill of materials (BOM) also contains components. Component identification, as actionable data, is important when it comes to defining the failure mode (Figure 2-7).

At work completion, the maintenance technician will know the failed component. These are typically the individual mechanical or electrical parts that fail.

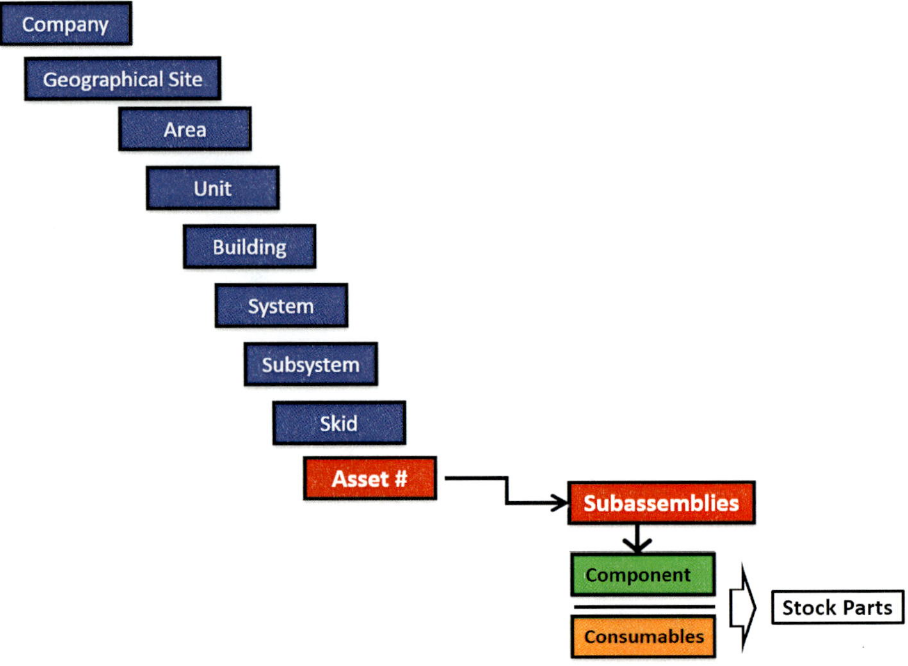

Figure 2-7: Identifying the component.

Examples of Assets and Their Components

Every equipment class (e.g., pump) has many, if not hundreds, of components (Figure 2-8). But these components are not necessarily in the item master registry. For example, the failed component might be the pump impeller; however, it may not be a stock part. Therefore, you cannot use the item master application as a source of this actionable data. Figure 2-8 shows components that could fail. Regarding the motor in the centrifugal pump system, if this is a large motor, it would be its own asset; otherwise, it's just a component.

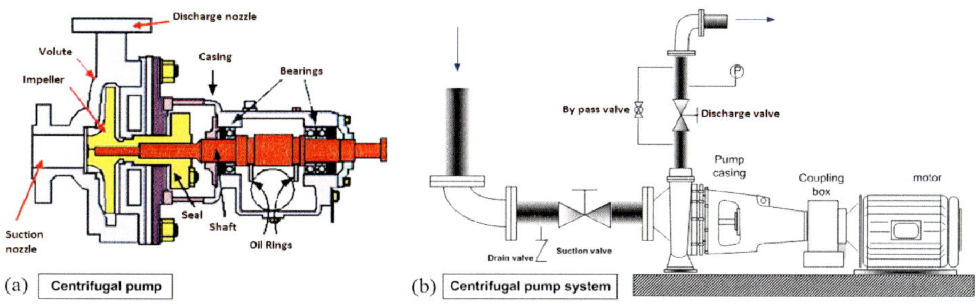

Figure 2-8: (a) A centrifugal pump and (b) pump system.

Understanding the Value in Analytical Reports

Analytical reports present data in a format that adds additional insight not readily apparent by looking at a single database record or even multiple records in a list. Using SQL (sequel query language) functions for line summaries, column totals, maximum/minimum values, or averages, the asset management team can identify large versus small, as well as outliers. SQL can also be used to perform groupings and then show larger (or smaller) values at the top, and stop after 10 records. This concept is very important in that management cannot stay on top of everything. Therefore, they want a database to display those worst offenders so that they can spend their time wisely. Analytical reports may also make use of graphical displays such as bar charts, histograms, and pie charts. Geographical information systems provide an additional way to look at tabular data using a map. An example of an SQL command is shown in Figure 2-9.

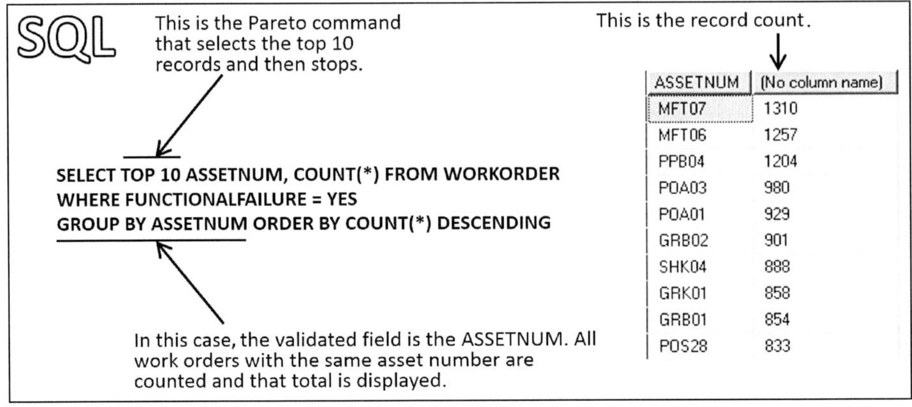

Figure 2-9: Example of SQL showing group by command.

KPI or Analytic: Which Is Best?

Key performance indicators are important for trending, but when management wants to know why, it helps to have the ability to drill down. This feature is typically provided with a dashboard or an analytical report. The analytical report can provide prompts which ask the user to specify filtering, group sorts, and dynamic drill-down capability. It is these analytical reports which will assist stakeholders in finding answers to critical problems and facilitate improvement.

Analytics Determine Input Requirements

One of the worst decisions any CMMS administrative team can make is to postpone the design (and creation) of analytical reports. Their thought process sometimes goes like this:

1. We have too much to do getting ready for go-live.
2. Foundation data is still being loaded.
3. Integrations need to be set up.
4. Roles need to be clarified.
5. CMMS operating procedures need to be documented.
6. Users need to be trained.

The problem with all of the above is the analytical report design may impact the design of the system. There is a good chance that new fields will be required, meaning they need to be added to the screen. Roles and process changes might also be identified. If pressed for time, you only have to document the report design at this early stage—not build it—to identify future input requirements. In summary, be sure to link outputs to inputs.

Advanced Analytics Provide Competitive Advantage

Creating powerful analytics can take time. Sometimes there are many design inputs to consider. Advanced functionality often leads to complexity. Final testing can also impact delivery time. All said, advanced analytic design enables the leadership to make more informed decisions. When sudden change occurs, management teams with the ability to quickly react by leveraging data are those that push ahead.

Advanced processes often involve advanced analytics. So as not to become overwhelmed with too much to do and remember, the best tactic is to create a long range plan. Examples of advanced processes include:

- RCM analysis
- Root cause analysis
- Chronic failure analysis
- Defect elimination
- Weekly scheduling
- Work Order feedback

Caution: Do not assume the out-of-the-box CMMS product will have the analytical reports you need.

Understanding Chronic Failure Analysis

Chronic Failure Analysis versus Root Cause Analysis

Chronic means recurring. These functional failures are not significant enough to warrant a root cause analysis. That said, they still need to be managed. By contrast, a root cause analysis is a significant review following a major event. Some organizations have documented trigger points that mandate the RCA. A root cause analysis "waits" for a major event to happen whereas the chronic failure analysis is a monthly review performed by the reliability team to identify the worst offenders and then drill down.

Design Considerations for Chronic Failure Analysis

There are several other considerations to keep in mind.

- The CMMS administrators must be clear on the definition of failure mode. Setting up a failure code hierarchy does not necessarily equate to a successful failure mode design.
- Every day that goes by without capturing a true failure mode is lost failure data never to be recovered. So an organization that delays this initiative 12 months will have to spend valuable time gleaning failure data from narrative text fields, or simply going with tribal knowledge.
- External software is sometimes used to store results of RCM analysis. This approach can be useful, but introduces additional software requiring integration, when the base product could be configured once the vision is clear.
- If this "external software" is just an Excel spreadsheet, it is highly unlikely that a living program will be supported.

Vision Must Be Clear

It is always best to design the system with the end game in mind. Quite often, the only goal for many organizations is to create work orders and capture actual costs. Cost management alone will not identify worst offenders. You may be able to identify the asset with the most cost, but you will not able to answer why. Therefore, the first step towards system optimization is to define how the CMMS should be set up to promote better decision making.

If deadlines are pressing, such as CMMS go-live, you may have to create a list of steps to perform afterwards. The question then becomes on what fields do we focus first? This answer will determine the time to extract value—some fields are more important than others.

Figure 2-10 illustrates a continuous improvement process for PM/CBT library refinement.

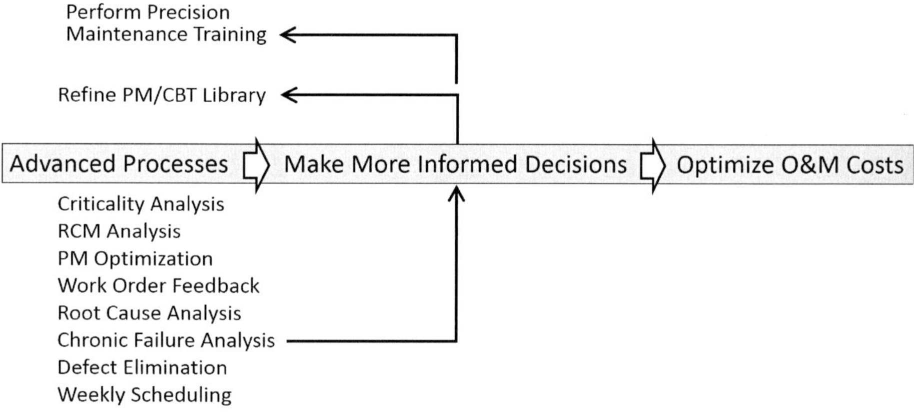

Figure 2-10: Continuous improvement process.

Below are key points to remember:

- 80% of all potential improvement is in the surrounding process and procedure.
- Advanced processes, although complex to set up, offer the largest potential return on investment. It's best to keep this in mind, as some organizations will pursue only the easy tasks.
- Chronic failure analysis, if performed, has the potential to identify 50% of all maintenance costs, per reliability expert Charles Latino. Some organizations write department procedures that say this role should populate the failure data at job completion. But that doesn't mean this procedure will guarantee complete and accurate updates.
- A reliability team can add value in many ways. They will be the administrators of the chronic failure analysis process.
- Once implemented, the asset offender report provides the reliability team the ability to identify worst offenders multiple ways and, once selected, drill down on failure modes. This report may very well determine the input field requirements. Lastly, do not assume the out-of-the-box CMMS has a decent failure analytic.
- A long range plan can pull together all improvement initiatives in a chronological order based on priority, risk, and benefit. This roadmap should be resource-leveled so that the staff can plan ahead and have a clear path to operational excellence.

A CMMS without failure data is merely a Work Order ticket system.

CHAPTER 3

Viewpoints from the RCM Facilitator

The Significance of Reliability Centered Maintenance

The purpose of reliability centered maintenance (RCM) is to provide a formal process for stakeholders to derive the optimum maintenance strategy for achieving higher degrees of safety, environmental integrity, and reliability, at minimal costs. By identifying probable failure modes, we can understand what, why, and how something might fail. We are then more likely to preempt that failure in the first place and minimize the consequences of failure.

Definition: RCM analysis is a systematic process for developing effective and applicable maintenance plans to preserve asset and system function by focusing on likely failure modes.

Definition: Reliability centered maintenance combines RCM analysis with the actual implementation, meaning the customer activates the maintenance strategy inside the CMMS.

We can determine the ideal maintenance strategy for inclusion in the CMMS in four ways:

1. RCM analysis
2. PM Optimization
3. OEM recommendations
4. Tribal knowledge

Understanding Asset Reliability

Reliability is not something that can be purchased or installed. To achieve high levels of reliability requires a comprehensive asset management plan. This plan includes RCM/PMO analysis. (PMO is preventive maintenance optimization, which generates a lot of failure modes primarily from the current maintenance program.) This structured approach helps organizations apply the right strategy at the right cost on the right asset. Further, an ideal design would seek continuous improvement through the use of feedback, thereby providing a "living program."

Very few people really understand reliability centered maintenance. It takes time and experienced people to perform a good RCM analysis. It should be performed on somewhere between 5–20% of your critical assets.

RCM consultant Douglas Plucknette, April 2014

What Is the Goal of RCM Analysis?

RCM analysis is intended to manage and minimize the probability of failure. The analysis is sometimes characterized as consisting of two sub-analyses: criticality analysis and FMEA (failure modes and effects analysis). The data generated by this analysis may be stored external to the CMMS. The CMMS administrators must then set up the necessary PM/CBT actions indicated by the analysis.

Failure mode analysis can be undertaken at any time in the life of an asset.

RCM Analysis Uses Seven Primary Questions

1. What are the functions and performance standards of the asset in its present operating context?
2. In what ways does it fail to fulfill its functions (functional failure) (Table 3-1)?

Table 3-1: Functional Failure

Function	Functional Failure
1. To maintain discharge flow of 500 gmp +/– 10%	A. Unable to discharge at all B. Discharge flow exceeds 550 gpm C. Discharge flow drops below 450 gpm

3. What causes each functional failure (failure modes)?
   The SAE JA1012 guideline recommends that "failure modes should be described in enough detail for it to be possible to select an appropriate failure management policy, but not in so much detail that excessive amounts of time are wasted on the analysis process itself."
4. What happens when each failure occurs (consequences)?
   - What will be observed when the failure occurs?
   - What is the impact on operations/production?
   - What is the impact on the environment/safety?
   - What physical change will occur to the equipment or adjacent equipment?
   - What alarms or indications will be observed?
5. In what way does each failure matter?
6. What can be done to predict or prevent each failure (maintenance tactic)?
7. What should be done if a suitable proactive task cannot be found?

What Is PM Optimization (PMO)?

The primary difference between RCM and PMO is the initial stage of the analysis; it relates to the way that failure modes are identified. RCM starts with a blank sheet of paper. It identifies the failure modes by first identifying the key functions required of the equipment (in its current operating context) and then the associated functional failures and failure modes. On the other hand, PMO uses existing preventive maintenance tasks and failure history to identify likely failure modes. In this sense, it tends to use current experience and practice as the starting point.

PMO closely evaluates each PM record (and tasks) by asking the following questions:

- What are the current PM tasks being performed?
- Are there duplicates? Is this PM properly worded? Are the task steps meaningful?
- Does the PM prevent or mitigate a failure? Can it be linked to a failure mode?
- Can the PM be replaced with CBT (condition based technology) or something non-intrusive?
- Is the asset less expensive to replace than maintain?
- Is the frequency valid?
- What failure history exists? What was the cause of failure?

What Is Meant by Criticality Analysis?

Criticality analysis of assets requires an objective assessment starting with system and sub-system breakdown. The criticality ranking is then determined by evaluating mission importance, operational consequence (repair cost and access to spare parts), and safety/environmental consequences. It is best done as a cross-functional group. Using this calculated result, RCM analysis is typically performed on the top 10–15% of critical assets. PM optimization is performed on the middle group of 70%, and OEM recommendations are used for the last 15%. The assumption is that criticality analysis is a prerequisite to RCM/PMO analysis.

Why Is RCM Analysis Sometimes Challenging?

As a reliability improvement initiative, RCM analysis can be challenging due to the skill sets involved, plant/system familiarity, the overall size of the effort, and cost. That said, a good RCM facilitator keeps the team focused and the process straightforward. More often than not, the primary hang-up occurs at the end of the project when the maintenance staff needs to implement the suggested tactic. Figure 3-1 shows the many reasons why RCM initiatives often fail.

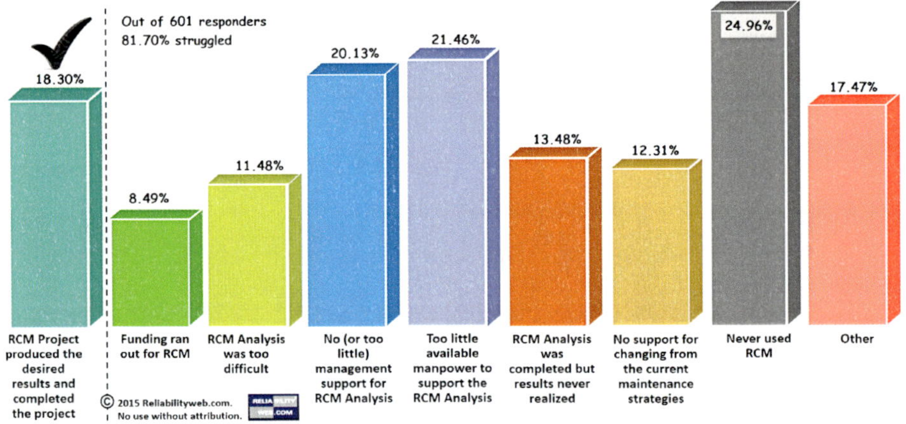

Figure 3-1: RCM initiatives often fail.

Multiple Definitions Exist within the RCM World

As with any complex subject there can be different definitions for the same term. Even the experts will disagree. It is up to the stakeholders to conduct their own research and find the definition that works best for them. For example, a failure mode can be defined as:

a. The ways, or modes, in which something might fail. (Uptime Elements FMEA passport)
b. Failures are any errors or defects, especially ones that affect the customer, and can be potential or actual. (American Society for Quality)
c. Manner in which equipment or a machine failure can occur. (Google)
d. Any single event, which causes a functional failure. (SAE JA-1012)

Regarding the definition, the most important thing is to choose one definition and stick to it. The above examples are all valid, but confusion arises when different groups choose to adopt different definitions.

Failure analysis can be performed different ways:

a. RCM analysis
b. PM optimization (PMO)
c. Failure modes effects analysis
d. Root cause analysis
e. Chronic failure analysis
f. Keyword search on the CMMS, looking for all past failures for that asset record
g. Conducting a conversation with the O&M technicians as to what happened

Table 3-2 summarizes how different books and standards define common RCM terms.

Table 3-2: Common RCM terms

	ATA MSG-3	NAVAIR	SAE JA1012	Moubray	FMEA
Function	The normal characteristic actions of an item	"An intended purpose of an item as described by a required standard of performance."	'What the owner or user of a physical asset or system wants it to do."	"A function statement should consist of a verb, an object, and a desired standard of performance."	A "function is what the item is intended to do, usually to a given standard of performance.

Table 3-2 Continued

	ATA MSG-3	NAVAIR	SAE JA1012	Moubray	FMEA
Functional Failure	Failure of an item to perform its intended function within specified limits	"The inability of an item to perform a specific function within the specified limits."	"A state in which a physical asset or system is unable to perform a specific function to a desired level of performance."	"A functional failure is defined as the inability of any asset to fulfil a function to a standard of performance which is acceptable to the user."	This term is not used in most applications of FMEA.
Failure Mode	Failure Mode is not defined. "Failure: the inability of an item to perform within previously specified limits."	"A specific physical condition that causes a functional failure. The failure mode statement should include a description of the failure mechanism (e.g., fatigue) whenever possible."	"A single event, which causes a functional failure."	"A failure mode is any event which causes a functional failure."	A "failure mode" is the manner in which the item or assembly could fail to meet the intended function and its requirements.

Table 3-2 Continued

	ATA MSG-3	NAVAIR	SAE JA1012	Moubray	FMEA
Failure Effect	What is the result of a functional failure?	"The result of a functional failure on surrounding items, the functional capability of the end item, and hazards to personnel and the environment."	"What happens when a failure mode occurs?"	"Failure Effects describe what happens when a failure mode occurs."	An "effect" is the consequence of the failure on the system or end-user.
Cause	Failure Cause: Why the functional failure occurs."	See above. "The failure mode statement should include a description of the failure mechanism (e.g. fatigue) whenever possible."	"Identify failure modes at a level of causation that makes it possible to identify an appropriate failure management policy."	"The level at which any failure mode should be identified is the level at which it is possible to identify an appropriate failure management policy."	A "cause" is the specific reason for the failure, preferably found by asking "why" until the root cause is determined.

The Role of the RCM Review Team

Figure 3-2 (a and b): Review team meeting.

Many RCM reviews are conducted with outside facilitators. Their skill set is quite specialized and they typically have years of experience. That said, a facilitator cannot perform this review without direct involvement by the customer. The review team is expected to have knowledge in the affected systems to be reviewed. Below is a list of additional requirements:

- Provide overall description of the system/equipment.
- Understand the case for doing the analysis and expected outcomes from this RCM analysis.
- Understand plant/facility operation of these assets.
- Bring P&IDs and engineering drawings to meeting room.
- Understand how this system relates to the organizational goals and what value it adds.
- Pull the failure history—whatever you have in whatever state it's in.
- Be aware of known issues with the equipment, including any RCAs
- Understand from the plant or block diagram where the system or equipment fits into the hierarchy.
- Have information about how much downtime costs per hour, minute, or day.
- Know the cost of new replacement.
- Provide spare part requirements.
- Identify the boundaries: what is included and what is excluded?
- Identify the alarms and interlocks.
- Provide information about major shutdowns, both planned and unplanned.

RCM Analysis and the CMMS Should Be Closely Connected

Many of the RCM, PMO, and FMEA programs commonly provided use different approaches. Although failure mode is the common language, it often has different interpretations. These differences in failure mode definition have led not only to confusion within the RCM community but also to an inability to clearly record this data within the CMMS product. Very seldom will you find a RCM practitioner who also has experience in CMMS implementation and optimization and vice versa.

To prove a point, ask this one question. Why hasn't the term *failure mode* been identified on the work order entry screen for capture at job completion so that this information could be readily compared to the RCM analysis maintenance strategy?

From a reliability standpoint, you need to know what failed, what went wrong, and what caused the failure to happen so that we can make an informed decision on what to do about it—or, in some cases, what not to do about it. Think of a world where, if you had accurate failure data, you could aggregate records and drill down on top offenders to discover causes. Somewhere along the way, we have overcomplicated the process and seem to be dancing around the CMMS (e.g., let's create an add-on software product which does failure analysis). Yet all we need to do is configure the CMMS and document the process.

Failure Mode Analysis: Determining the Right Level of Detail

New facilitators (and customers) often struggle with the amount of detail. However, consider this: you only need to analyze to the level of depth that will enable your analysis team to arrive at a maintenance tactic that lets you manage that single failure mode.

System Criticality Is a Factor

The level of detail also depends on system criticality. For example, when analyzing the failure mode "Printed circuit board fails," the maintenance tactic might be simply to replace with the board with a new one. But for a critical asset, you may need to analyze down to the level where an individual diode failure occurs within the circuit board. Perhaps this is part of a military system where mission failure could have catastrophic effects. That said, if you start analyzing every diode on a circuit board, you will be analyzing for a very, very long time. If the end result of that diode failure is ten minutes of downtime (that does not lead to a loss of production), then this failure mode would be given a low priority.

A Common Sense Strategy for Failure Analysis

If you analyze everything at the same level of detail, your analysis will not be complete or it will be so bloated that it will take too long to complete. The effects of such an extended, seemingly never-ending analysis on the team performing this work can also be seriously damaging to your efforts. This has often been referred to as "analysis paralysis." Therefore, you should start at a high level of analysis and drill down as and when needed. If an analysis starts at too low a level, you will end up in a rabbit hole! You can always go deeper, but once you are in a deep hole, it can be difficult to find your way out.

Prebuilt Failure Mode Lists: Do They Add Value?

Over the past twenty years, quite a few failure mode libraries have been created with the goal of speeding up the RCM process. Prebuilt failure mode lists usually consist of a complete sentence containing the component, component problem, and cause code. These prebuilt failure mode lists are often sold as a package and usually linked to other software outside the CMMS. In the end, you have a database external to the CMMS, which adds integration complexity and makes it less likely to be updated over time.

Prebuilt Lists Sound Catchy

Prebuilt failure mode lists sound catchy and probably help the sales pitch by promising quicker and easier analysis. However, this pitch causes the consumer to falsely believe the list is ready to go. It may have thousands of records, but it is very unlikely to be an exact match for your industry or systems. Consequently, your review team must first focus on the list and not the component. Therein, too much time is spent sifting through a canned list and not thinking about likely failure modes for your operating context.

Sifting through Data

Because clicking your way through this type of list can be very long and time consuming, the RCM review team cannot easily single out the component or component problem they have in mind. Many times the list contains phrases that are totally irrelevant. Even though these lists may be divided by asset classification, they are still quite unwieldy. Quite often, the RCM facilitator and analysis team are pulled into non-relevant discussions, wasting time when they could be focusing only on the components of interest to them.

Facilitators State Their Opinion

Most RCM facilitators say that this prebuilt list search-and-find process:

1. Slows down the RCM analysis;
2. Discourages the review team from focusing on the P&ID drawings;
3. Reduces buy-in to the final product (by not creating something of their own); and worse yet,
4. Encourages maintenance tasks to be inserted for failures that would never occur in their current operating context.

Basically, you end up with two reviews: a Day One review (clean-up) of the entire list, and then the time you spend searching for the next component. The prebuilt list is essentially controlling the conversation as opposed to the analysis team being guided by the RCM facilitator.

Note: Facilitators may still have access to such libraries in order to make sure the analysis team has covered what is needed.

Identifying the Single Event Failure Mode

It is the goal of RCM facilitators to seek out the single event. By their very definition, single events happen alone, but they can be part of a chain of events. If you are at the root cause single event, the other events happen only as part of the effects chain (Figure 3-3). It is important to distinguish the single event failure mode from the failure effects. Experienced facilitators are well aware of the pitfalls that can mistakenly identify effects as causes.

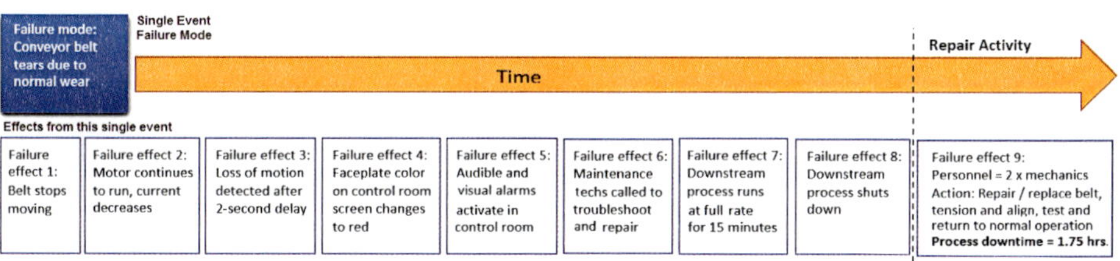

Figure 3-3: Single event failure mode and the effects chain.

A facilitator—asking an analysis team the open-ended question, "Why does the conveyor fail?"—may be flooded with ideas in quick succession from the team members. For example, the facilitator may hear in rapid succession: "Motor fails," "Belt rips,"

"No power," "Operator shuts it down," "Overload," "Feed chute plugged," "Product too heavy," and "Gearbox broken." This kind of information overload can be daunting, but experienced facilitators must be skilled to deal with these situations.

Sample Failure Modes

What are the reasons a motor can fail? Possible answers include the following:

- Motor bearing fails due to lube failure.
- Motor bearing fails due to false brinelling.
- Motor fails due to short circuit.
- Motor fails due to open circuit.
- Motor is damaged by water ingress.
- Motor power cables are damaged by impact.
- Motor electrical connections are loose due to installation error.

Caution: Failure to discern the actual cause of failure could easily lead teams to create maintenance tasks that could be ineffective and potentially expensive, without realizing it once the RCM decision logic is applied, or to oversimplify and enter "motor fails."

RCM Analysis Spreadsheets

Many RCM facilitators make use of an Excel spreadsheet. A typical RCM analysis spreadsheet might have columns labeled as follows:

A	B	C	D	E
Function	Functional Failure	Failure Mode	Failure Effects	Maintenance Tactic
Function	Functional Failure	Failure Mode	Failure Effects	Maintenance Tactic

Additional notes:

1. There will be multiple functions.
2. There will be multiple functional failures per function.
3. There will be multiple failure modes per functional failure.
4. There will be a single task associated with each failure mode.

Like the CMMS work order entry screen, the spreadsheet can have validated fields to help build the failure mode. Free format text is still useful, but some fields need to be validated so they can be used for aggregating data in analytical reports.

When the failure mode is pulled together, it reads as:

FailedComponent	ComponentProblem	"due to"	CauseCode

Failure Mode Has Three Parts

Figure 3-4 is an illustration from RCM Facilitator Douglas Plucknette. Typical CMMS design has the work order linked to the asset (pump) with a problem description and asset problem code (noise). Most reliability engineers would agree, however, that proper failure analysis requires the failed component, component problem, and cause code.

Note: Some RCM experts define Failure Mode as just the failed component and problem code.

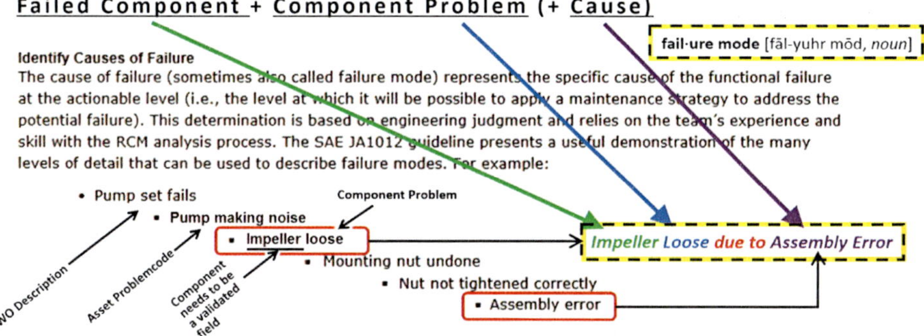

Figure 3-4: The three parts of a failure mode.

RCM Decision Logic

An RCM decision tree looks at safety, operational, non-operational, and hidden failure consequences. The resultant decision might involve a time-directed task, condition monitoring task, run to failure, or redesign.

The decision tree in Figure 3-5 begins with a fundamental question, determining whether a failure is evident to the operators under normal procedures. A hidden failure leads to a series of other questions under the category of hidden failure consequences.

If the failure is evident, the next determining factor is whether the failure has safety consequences. A positive answer leads to its own series of questions. If safety is not a factor, the next consideration is whether the consequences of the failure are operational or non-operational. Each series of questions leads to a potential type of task. The decision tree is also organized to help you identify whether the impact of the failure is immediate or delayed.

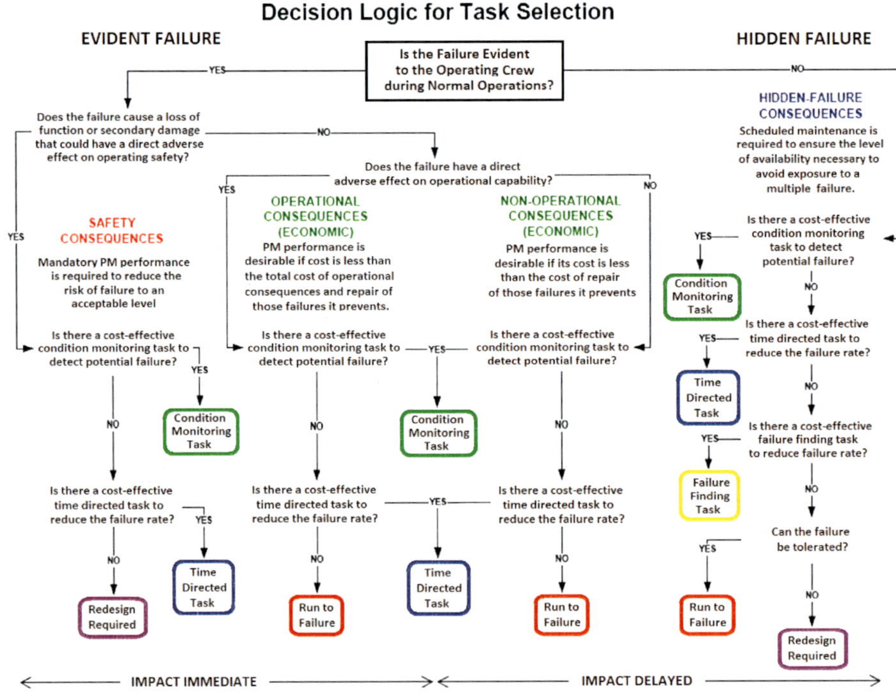

Figure 3-5: An RCM decision tree.

Applicable and Effective Task Creation

A common error that inexperienced facilitators make is to follow the RCM decision logic and create a task simply because it is applicable and technically feasible—but then forget about how effective that task may be. In other words, it may be possible to create a task, but that task may not make sense in terms of economics or effectively managing the safety or environmental risk.

Suppose the team decides that a particular condition-based task is applicable for a particular failure mode. It will cost $2k per year to detect the onset of a failure where the MTBF is 5 years. This total PM cost ($10k) should be compared to the total cost of breakdown (Figure 3-6). In this case, the task should be rejected because the cost of $10k is considerably higher than the cost of a breakdown ($3k). It is important to remember that the actual failure is not being avoided. It is going to occur whether or not you spend money to detect it.

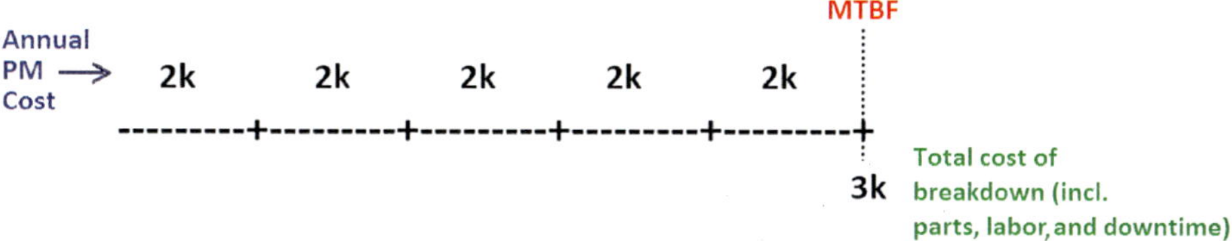

Figure 3-6: Evaluating costs.

What Is Needed to Make a Solid Decision?

For any failure mode that results in an unacceptable safety or environmental risk, you will be dealing with the definition of what is acceptable or tolerable to the asset owner as well as ensuring compliance with any regulatory requirements that might apply. This sounds pretty straightforward but, in reality, it can be quite difficult to pin down. Many organizations struggle with risk management. They assume that, if they have performed a criticality assessment, their risks are managed. Although a solid criticality assessment is needed to identify the high risk assets, the assessment does not tell you how to manage those risks.

Criticality is a foundational tool to identify which assets or systems need to be addressed to control risks. It helps prioritize the necessary tools and resources. This is true whether the risks are identified as having environmental, safety, or economic consequences.

The RCM Maintenance Tactic

RCM analysis has five possible outcomes: RTF (run to failure), time or usage-based, redesign, redundancy, and real time monitoring. In turn, the time or usage-based activity has five options (Figure 3-7).

This exact same failure mode coding from the RCM facilitation is used by the CMMS work order failure coding. This key design element should be recognized. The primary objective for each failure mode is to identify a suggested maintenance tactic.

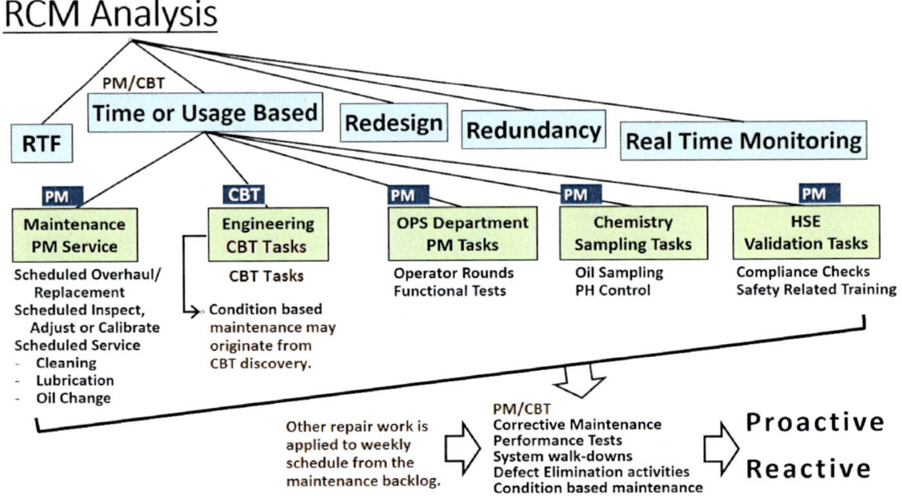

Figure 3-7: RCM analysis outcomes.

Significance of the Failure Mode

Table 3-3 compares incorrect and correct failure modes. The failure mode definition must include the following:

1. What is it? (the component)
2. What happened to it? (the event or problem)
3. Why did it happen? (the cause)

More information than that covered by these three questions will potentially be confusing. Conversely, less information may not be enough to drive maintenance decisions correctly.

Table 3-3: Correct and Incorrect Failure Modes

Type of Failure Mode	Example
INCORRECT It is difficult to see exactly what is being identified as the object or what happened to it. The failure team uses too much jargon and their answer does not meet the definition of failure mode. Multiple causes of failure seem to occur in this example, mixed with failure effects. If failure modes are recorded in this way, interfacing the data with a CMMS system will be difficult.	Position of the LLHR in DCD label packet not identified by general engineering and "Requirement in Purchase Specification" for mousepad, but not identified on Bill of Material and LICD Card content requirements not identified in Build Procedure.
CORRECT Failure modes should be succinct and address only single events.	• Conveyor drive belt tears due to wear.

Simplifying the Format

Translating between different recording methodologies does not have to be difficult. For example, the data in Table 3-4a may not meet your needs, but it can be easily converted to a simpler format, as shown in Table 3-4b.

Table 3-4 (a and b): Recording the Failure Mode

FMEA Ref.	Item	Potential Failure Mode	Potential Cause(s) / Mechanism
1.1.1.1	Brake manifold Ref. Designator 2b, Channel A, O-ring	Internal Leakage From Channel A to B	a) O-ring Compression Set (Creep) failure b) surface damage during assembly

Failure Mode	Failure Effects
1.1.1.1 Brake manifold O-ring (Designator 2b, Channel A) Compression set creep	Internal leakage from channel A to channel B

Another example of converted data is shown in Figure 3-5, where Table 3-5a is converted to the simpler format of Table 3-5b.

Table 3-5 (a and b): Another Example of Recording the Failure Mode

Potential Failure Mode	Potential Effect of Failure	Potential Causes of Failure
Output stuck high or low	Instruments show zero readout	Short circuit caused by insufficient space between conductors

Failure Mode	Failure Effects
Short circuit cause by insufficient space between conductors	Output stuck high or low. Instruments show zero readout.

Failure Effects

Failure effects detail what happens when the associated failure mode occurs. They should tell the story from the onset of failure until the equipment (and therefore function) is fully restored. For RCM analyses, the effects are recorded as if nothing is currently being done to prevent or detect the failure.

Example of Failure Effects

As the belt wears over time, it will eventually break. The drive motor continues to run, but motor current decreases. The loss of conveyor motion is detected, which shuts off power to the motor after approximately 2 seconds. The loss of motion alarm activates in the control room. The faceplate color for the conveyor system in the control room display will change to red and an audible warning will activate. The downstream process can be run at a reduced rate for up to 15 minutes. After this period, processing will be shut down. Downtime costs 2 hours to replace the belt, tension, align, and restart processing. Personnel requirements call for 2 mechanics.

CHAPTER 4

Configuring the System

There's a saying, "Multiple consultants can have multiple answers to the same question." Assuming the CMMS can be easily configured, it is quite possible for different approaches to be taken. Whatever the final choice, the stakeholders must be sure they can reach their stated goals.

How Would the Failure Mode Be Captured?

There Are Multiple Ways to Capture the Failed Component (in the CMMS)

1. You can add new fields for component, component problem, and cause code. Each field can have its own domain (value list).
2. Similar to Option 1, you can create a new classification record with three levels (Failure class, Mechanical/Electrical, and Component). This would be in place of adding a new component field with a domain.
3. You can hijack an existing application field (if unused) displayed on the Work Order screen and set up to store failure data.

The option I do not recommend is the utilization of a failure code hierarchy to store the failure mode data (explained later), as this becomes unwieldy.

Option 1: Add New Failure Data Fields to Work Order

Within the CMMS, you have a Work Order creation screen (Figure 4-1). In the life of the Work Order, it is best to capture failure data (which includes the failure mode) at Work Order completion. The responsibility for entry might be different for every organization, but a possible scenario might be:

1. Failed component by the maintenance technician,
2. Component problem by the maintenance supervisor, and
3. Cause code by the reliability engineer.

Note: Failure data is required only on repair work where a functional failure has occurred. Functional failure should also drive MTBF calculations.

The shaded fields at the bottom of Figure 4-1 would enable the failure analytic report to drill down on the failure mode.

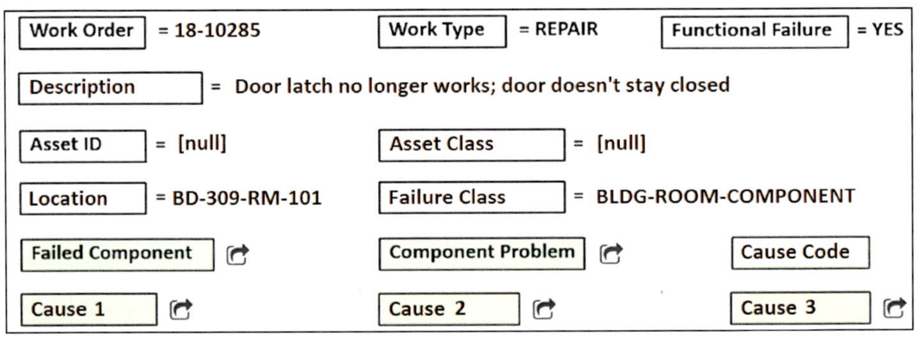
Work Order = 18-10285
Work Type = REPAIR
Functional Failure = YES
Description = Door latch no longer works; door doesn't stay closed
Asset ID = [null]
Asset Class = [null]
Location = BD-309-RM-101
Failure Class = BLDG-ROOM-COMPONENT
Failed Component
Component Problem
Cause Code
Cause 1
Cause 2
Cause 3

Figure 4-1: CMMS Work Order Creation Screen.

Setting Up a Component List

Figure 4-2 shows a sample component list. Depending on the definition of asset criteria, components on this list may actually be assets. This component list is determined by the failure class.

Pump

- Balancing drum
- Bearing
- Casing
- Controls
- Coupling
- Cylinder/casing/liner
- Diaphragm
- Impeller
- Lubricator
- Mechanical seal
- Piston
- Rotor
- Rotor assembly
- Shaft
- Valves
- Wear rings

Elec Generator

- Air filter
- Bearing, radial
- Bearing, thrust
- Cooling system
- Exciter
- Lube system
- Protective system
- Rotor
- Stator

Boilers

- Air/water supply
- Burners
- Controls
- Elec heating elements
- Fuel system
- Furnace tubing
- Insulation/lining
- Pressure parts
- Valves

Gas Turbines

- Air compressor
- Air filter
- Bearing
- Blades
- Burners/combustors
- Casing
- Controls
- Coupling
- Fire protection system
- Fuel gas supply
- Fuel oil supply
- Gas generator
- Gear box
- Lube system
- Power turbine
- Starting unit
- Ventilation fan

Door

- Armature plate
- Astragal center
- Body
- Closure device
- Crashbar
- Door knob/Lockset
- Frame/Casing
- Glass
- Hinge
- Lock jamb
- Sweep
- Threshold/Sill
- Vestibule
- Weather stripping

Figure 4-2: Sample component list.

Setting Up Component Problem Codes

A generic problem code list can be created which fits the majority of all asset classifications (Figure 4-3). This same problem code list can be applied to either the asset or the component, as both are needed. I also prefer to have some "intelligence" built into the code itself to make it easier to select and use inside failure reporting. When building the problem code description, the administrator joins together the individual problem codes in column A (or column D, etc.) to make one long description separated by a special character (e.g., semi-colon or back-slash). An example is CALIB with a description of "Miss-Cal-Stick; Out-of-Cal; Out-of-Spec." This approach links together similar problem codes to give us a standard set of validated codes.

A	B	D	E	G	H	J	K
BALANCE	Out of Balance	ERODED	Corroded	INSTALLATION	Not-needed	OVERHEAT	Burned-out
CALIB	Miss-Cal-Stick	ERODED	Eroded	INSTALLATION	Wrong	OVERHEAT	Fire
CALIB	Out-of-Cal	ERODED	Pitted	INSTALLATION	Backward	OVERHEAT	Over Temperature
CALIB	Out-of-Spec	FLUIDS	Level-Bad	INTERNAL	Cavitation	OVERHEAT	Smoke
CONTAMINATEI	Contaminated	FLUIDS	Mix-Bad	INTERNAL	Improper-Flow	PESTS	Deceased
DAMAGE	Abrasion	FORM	Bent-Sagging	INTERNAL	Seat-Leak	PESTS	Infestation
DAMAGE	Broken	FORM	Collapsed-Buckled	LEAKING	Dripping	PESTS	Unwanted
DAMAGE	Chafed-Galling	FORM	Ductile	LIGHTING	Dim	PRESSURE	Over/Under Pressure
DAMAGE	Chipped	FORM	Brittle	LIGHTING	Flickering	SEIZED	Binding
DAMAGE	Cracked	FORM	Fatigued	LIGHTING	Light-out	SEIZED	Jammed
DAMAGE	Cut-Sheared-Torn	FORM	Leaning	MISSING	Missing	SEIZED	Frozen
DAMAGE	Delaminated	FORM	Warped	MISSING	Lost	SEIZED	Locked-up
DAMAGE	Deteriorated	FORM	Melted	MISALIGNED	Equip-misaligned	SEIZED	Seized
DAMAGE	Discolored	FORM	Twisted	NOISE	Abnormal-sound	SEIZED	Stuck
DAMAGE	Disintegrated	FOULED	Blocked	NOISE	Hitting	SEPARATED	Disconnected
DAMAGE	Exploded-Shattered	FOULED	Clogged	NOISE	Make-Contact	SEPARATED	Loose
DAMAGE	Fractured	FOULED	Dirty	NOISE	Rubbing	SEPARATED	Separated
DAMAGE	Frayed	FOULED	Plugged			SEPARATED	Unbonded
DAMAGE	Graffiti	FOULED	Slag-buildup	POWER-ELEC	Abnormal-Current	SEPARATED	Weak-Tension
DAMAGE	Nicked-Notched	FUNCTION	Defective	POWER-ELEC	Blown	SEPARATED	Split
DAMAGE	Pipewall-Weak	FUNCTION	INOP-Stopped	POWER-ELEC	Discharged-Nocharge	SMELL	Bad-odor
DAMAGE	Punctured	FUNCTION	Intermittent	POWER-ELEC	Ground-Fault	TEMPCTRL	Low-heat-xfer
DAMAGE	Rotting	FUNCTION	Open	POWER-ELEC	No-connection	TEMPCTRL	TooCold
DAMAGE	Ruptured	FUNCTION	Ops-not-to-spec	POWER-ELEC	No-Start	TEMPCTRL	TooHot
DAMAGE	Scratched-Scored	FUNCTION	Overstress	POWER-ELEC	Open-circuit	TEMPCTRL	Will-not-cool
DAMAGE	Worn	FUNCTION	Overload	POWER-ELEC	Overload	VIBRATION	Excessive-Vibe
DISPLAY	Alarming	FUNCTION	Poor-Prod-Rate	POWER-ELEC	Shorted		
DISPLAY	Bad-Reading	FUNCTION	Raise-Lower-Problem	POWER-ELEC	Spark-Arc	LEAKING	External Leak
DISPLAY	False Indication	FUNCTION	Speed-Control	POWER-ELEC	Tripped	LEAKING	Spilling
DISPLAY	Fluctuates	FUNCTION	Unstable			LEAKING	Spray
DISPLAY	Incorrect						
DISPLAY	Sensor-bad						

Figure 4-3: Standard 26 Problem Codes.

The problem code list in Figure 4-3 can be enhanced to reflect your industry and may grow in size. The problem code is the first observation by the technician or operator as to an abnormal event. The component problem code is specific to the failed component.

Setting Up a Cause Code List

This topic applies to CMMS cause codes. Strategies for capturing cause codes include:

1. Identify and store all cause codes on the CMMS work order record.
2. Identify and store all cause codes on the CMMS investigation application.
3. Identify and store all cause codes on software external to CMMS.

Whatever cause codes are used, the answer must be precise enough to analyze chronic (recurring) failures. Because there are so many possible cause fields for a given failure event, the design in Figure 4-4 is used to create smaller lists by starting at a higher level and ending at lower level.

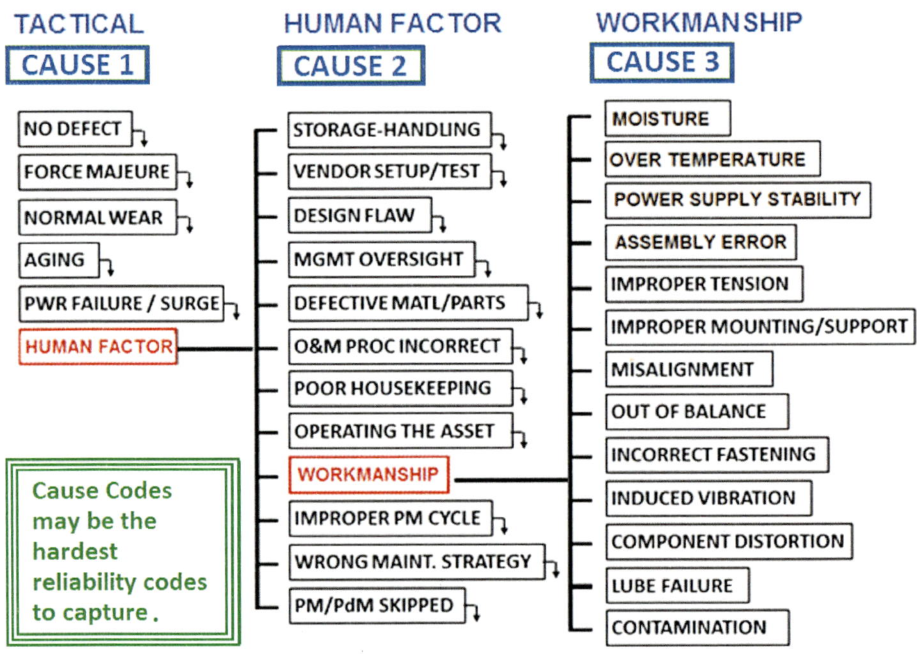

Figure 4-4: A drill-down methodology for finding the true cause.

These three cause fields are answered from left to right. It's possible you may stop with Cause 1 or Cause 2. But if a red box is chosen, the next cause field must be filled in. For example, if workmanship is chosen for Cause 2, a value in Cause 3 must be entered. The failure mode will use the last entry from wherever you stop entering values. These three fields are accessible from the Work Order record. *Note:* In the case where this is a critical asset involving a recurring problem, it is wise for the leadership to investigate the systemic or latent causes—which are stored in a separate field (called Cause 4).

Systemic or Latent Failure Analysis is Sometimes Required

The component can fail, but the component itself is not normally why anything fails. Winston Ledet, a widely known consultant and instructor on proactive maintenance, discovered that up to 84 percent of equipment failures can be linked to human factors. There are different cause categories—tactical, human influence and workmanship. Within human factors are systemic and latent causes. Analysis of this type might require a one-on-one conversation led by the maintenance manager. The objective is to find out how we can truly prevent this event from happening again (Figure 4-5).

Systemic and latent causes are concealed or hidden causes; they eventually cause human error to be committed. Poorly defined procedures and roles can induce failures. Latent cause analysis looks at system flaws, procedure omissions, organizational weaknesses (e.g., no reliability engineer), and flawed management decisions.

Note: There can be more than one root cause.

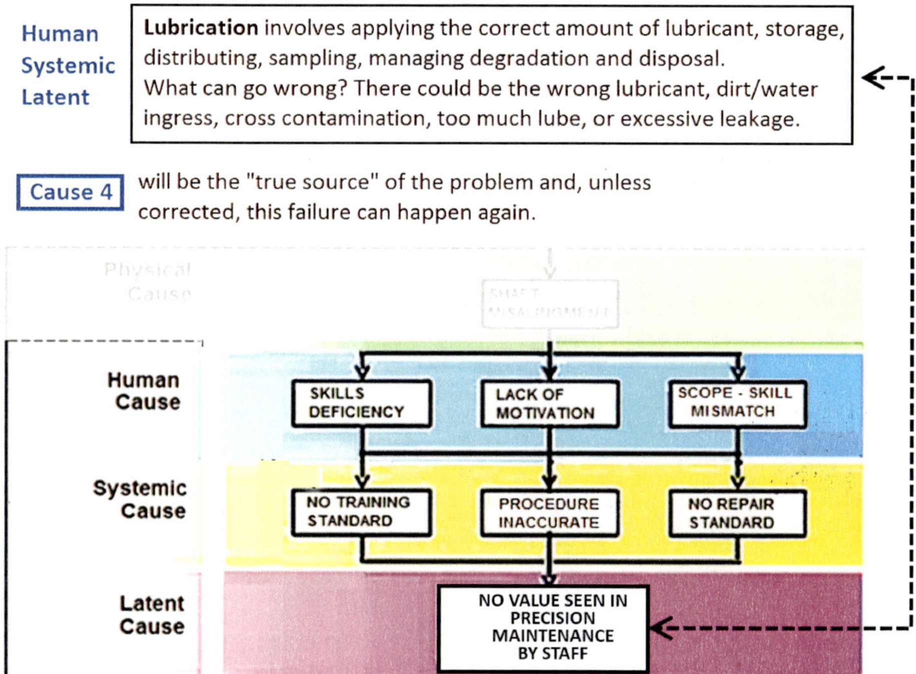

Figure 4-5: System or latent failure analysis.

Formal root cause analysis (RCA) goes into this detail for every investigation. But it may not be practical to go to this level of detail for every functional failure in the CMMS. That said, there should be a process to focus on those bad actors that represent the majority of all problems. Using a Pareto analysis technique, stakeholders will know where to start, i.e., what assets to focus on and what failure modes to drill down on. This starting point list might also be influenced by critical assets, assets on a watch list, or selected asset classifications. Once the failure mode is apparent, the reliability engineer performing the investigation will dive much deeper into failure mechanisms and latent causes. Figure 4-6 provides a sample breakout for mechanical and electrical failure mechanisms.

Failure Mechanisms

- For **Mechanical**
  - Erosion
  - Fatigue
  - Overload
  - Corrosion
    - Concentration cell corrosion
    - Stress corrosion cracking
    - Chloride stress cracking
    - Dezincification
- For **Electrical**
  - Overload due to supply transient
  - Overload due to load stall
  - Electrical equivalent of fatigue
  - Insulation breakdown due to heat
  - Insulation breakdown due to UV radiation
  - Insulation breakdown due to chemical attack
  - Mechanical loosening

Figure 4-6: Sample failure mechanisms.

Option 2: Utilize Classification Field to Store Component

With the Classification field, the users can drill down through the categories to arrive at the failed component. If the component is not in the list, they can enter it in the Suggested Add field. The software can be configured to automatically rout this suggested value to appropriate staff for review. Once approved, the software automatically inserts the new record in the classification hierarchy and updates the Work Order. These fields are shown in Figure 4-7.

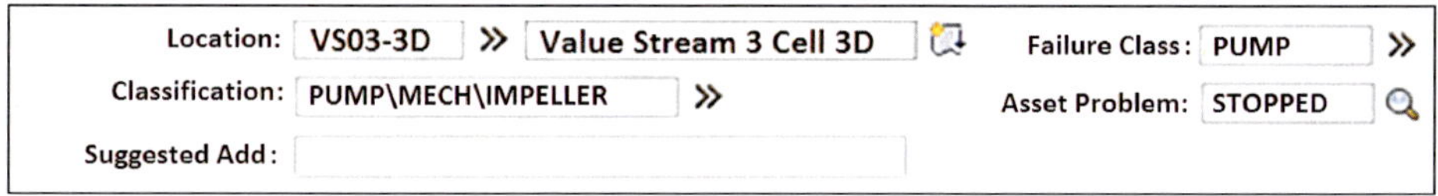

Figure 4-7: Showing use of Classification field to store the failed component.

Option 3: Hijack Existing (Unused) Fields

Figure 4-8 shows the failure mode being stored in existing—but unused—fields. For example, the failed component is stored in the Configuration field; the component problem is stored in the Classification field; and the cause code is stored in the Launch Entry field.

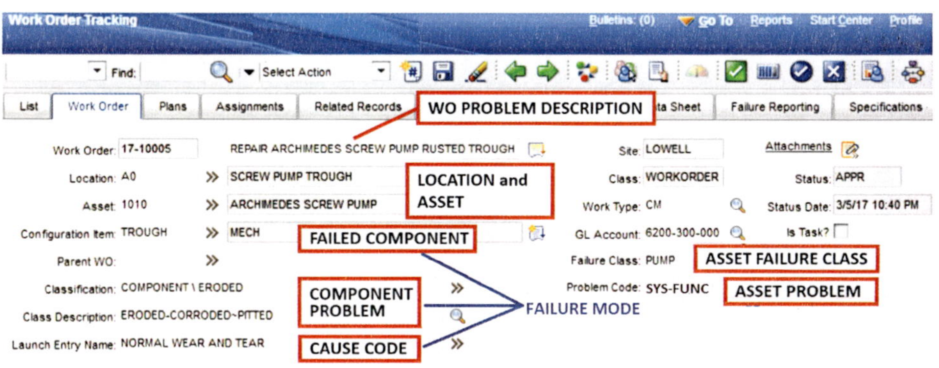

Figure 4-8: Work Order tracking unused fields.

Storing Failure Mode on the Work Order

As previously shown, the failure mode data can be stored in multiple ways on the Work Order screen. The three pieces of the failure mode—failed component, component problem, and cause code—are brought together during the run time of the asset offender report.

Figure 4-9 shows how we capture the failure mode using new fields on the Work Order. In this case, the Classification field is used for storing the failed component. But the Component Problem, Remedy, and Cause fields are new. *Note:* If the Classification field is already in use for your Work Order tracking application, then you can use an alternative design, but achieve the same results in terms of selecting components.

The entry in the Component Problem field is "Separated." The domain for this field is the same standard 26 problem codes that are used for the Asset Problem code.

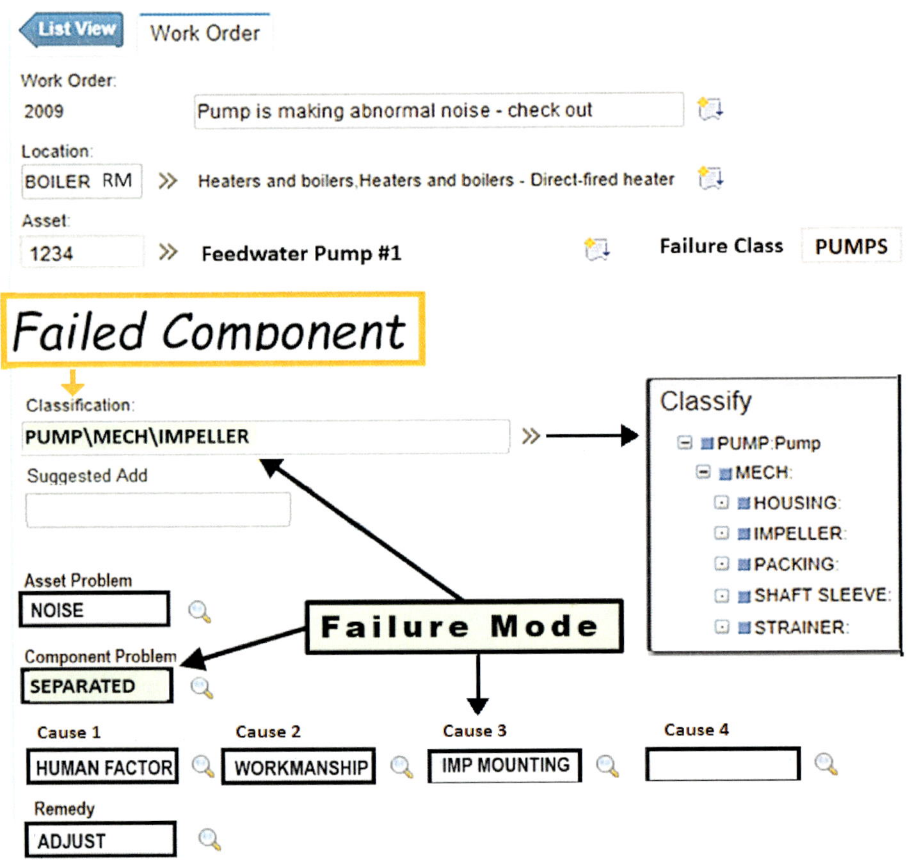

Figure 4-9: Capturing the failure mode.

The Suggested Add Field

The component list will most likely be built over time. Creating a "suggested add" field makes it extremely easy for the maintenance technicians to type (in free format text) whatever component is missing from the list. This feature makes the process of capturing missing components user friendly.

Set Up the Asset Offender Report (AOR)

What Makes a Good Failure Analytic?

1. Multiple prompts presenting multiple processing options
2. A wealth of information
3. Dynamic drill-down capability

The best type of analytical reports allow for dynamic drill down. This means that the user is allowed to enter additional parameters to control the focus and display more detail. Quite often they are asking questions like, "Why is this?" and "What is causing this trend?"

Users can run the Asset Offender Report six different ways (Pareto groups). In addition they can filter on plant system, asset classification, criticality, manufacturer, or date range. By choosing a specific asset number, they can drill down into failure mode data (components, problems, and causes) displayed as pie charts. These different options allow the monthly meeting coordinator to lead the analysis in multiple directions.

Sample Layout

Figure 4-10 shows a sample layout of an Asset Offender Report. This Pareto-style failure analytic, developed using Maximo, empowers decision makers, enabling them to identify the worst offenders and then manage by exception. (Maximo is an enterprise asset management system available from IBM.)

The upper right of the figure lists several filter options. This particular report has been sorted using the Column Sort (Prompt 1). These columns are the seven columns on the right side of the report. Six of the seven (with the blue arrows) are the possible sorts: number of (WO failures), MTBF days, asset condition, downtime, percent purchase, and age. The percent purchase column measures the average cost (see the annual average cost column) divided by the replacement cost, shown as a percentage.

This sample report indicates ten at-risk assets, with Asset EN0012, one of the compressors, being the asset most at risk.

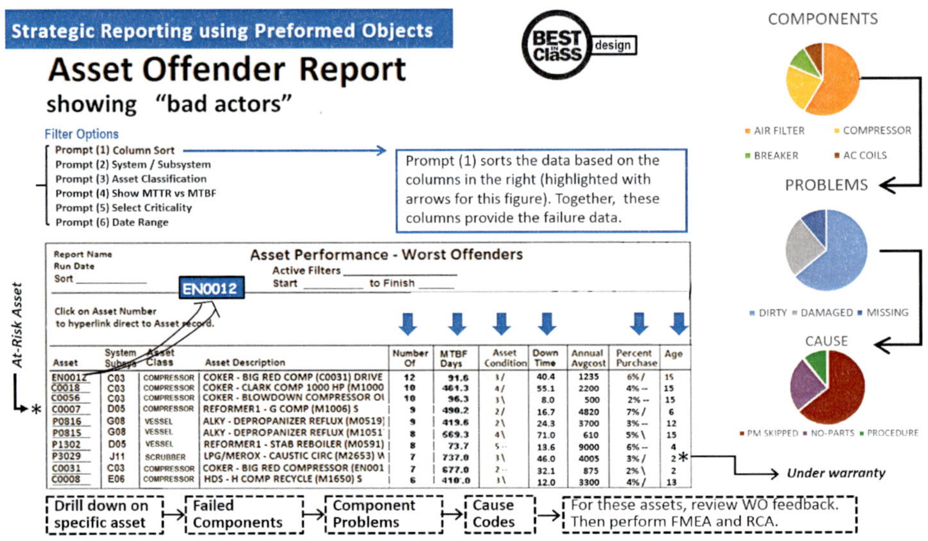

Asset	System Subsys	Asset Class	Asset Description	Number Of	MTBF Days	Asset Condition	Down Time	Annual Avgcost	Percent Purchase	Age
EN0012	C03	COMPRESSOR	COKER - BIG RED COMP (C0031) DRIVE	12	91.6	3 /	40.4	1235	6% /	15
C0018	C03	COMPRESSOR	COKER - CLARK COMP 1000 HP (M1000	10	461.3	4 /	55.1	2200	4% --	15
C0056	C03	COMPRESSOR	COKER - BLOWDOWN COMPRESSOR OI	10	96.3	3 \	8.0	500	2% --	15
C0007	D05	COMPRESSOR	REFORMER1 - G COMP (M1006) S	9	490.2	2 /	16.7	4820	7% /	6
P0816	G08	VESSEL	ALKY - DEPROPANIZER REFLUX (M0519)	9	419.6	2 \	24.3	3700	3% --	12
P0815	G08	VESSEL	ALKY - DEPROPANIZER REFLUX (M1051	8	669.3	4 \	71.0	610	5% \	15
P1302	D05	VESSEL	REFORMER1 - STAB REBOILER (M0591)	8	73.7	5 --	13.6	9000	6% --	4
P3029	J11	SCRUBBER	LPG/MEROX - CAUSTIC CIRC (M2653) W	7	737.0	3 \	46.0	4005	3% /	2*
C0031	C03	COMPRESSOR	COKER - BIG RED COMPRESSOR (EN001	7	677.0	2 --	32.1	875	2% \	2
C0008	E06	COMPRESSOR	HDS - H COMP RECYCLE (M1650) S	6	410.0	3 \	12.0	3300	4% /	13

Figure 4-10: Sample layout of an Asset Offender Report.

Other Report Features

1. Any at-risk assets could be tagged as a (Maximo) bookmark. In Figure 4-10, Asset C0007 has been bookmarked.
2. Assets still under warranty will have an asterisk in the age column. In Figure 4-10, Asset P3029, which is 2 years old, is still under warranty.
3. You can filter on asset classification or criticality.
4. You can replace MTBF with MTTR as a filter.
5. You can filter by manufacturer.
6. You can restrict the date range.
7. You can also multiply Asset Criticality times Asset Condition to provide an additional Pareto-sort option.

Tips and Tricks

By adding the new fields shown in yellow in Figure 4-11, you can quickly calculate the average annual maintenance cost (divided by asset replacement cost).

Asset Main Entry Screen

YTD COST
TOTAL COST
These fields are beneficial to those who want to track budget values.

LAST 12 MONTHS
LAST 12-24 MONTHS
LAST 24-36 MONTHS
If populated, these fields would enable the quick calculation of **Average Annual Maintenance Costs** when running the Asset Offender Report. A weekly routine could be set up to perform this calculation, which resets these values.

Figure 4-11: Adding new fields.

Storing RCM Analysis Results inside the CMMS

Tip: It is a best practice to have the PM/CBT library linked to the failure modes and maintenance tactics.

Figure 4-12 shows a typical design for RCM analysis, with this medium outside the CMMS. Third-party software has an extra cost.

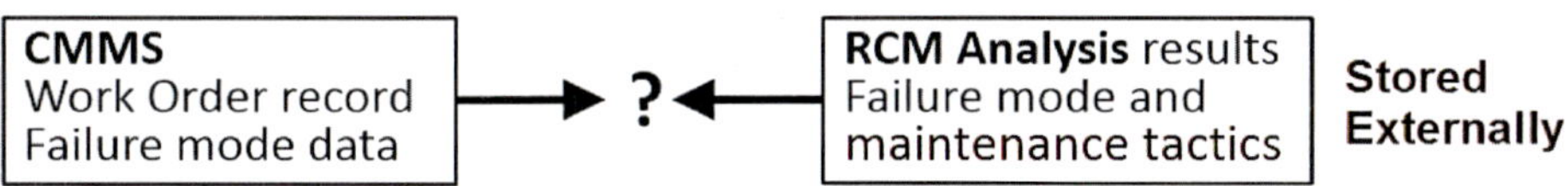

Figure 4-12: RCM analysis design.

Internal Design Supports a "Living Program"

From an ease-of-use perspective, it would be advantageous to store RCM results directly inside the CMMS as a new application (Figure 4-13). Trying to perform periodic improvements to the RCM analysis stored outside the CMMS can be difficult. Furthermore, when these two entities are separate from each other, there is no guarantee the asset identifiers or failure mode data will synch up.

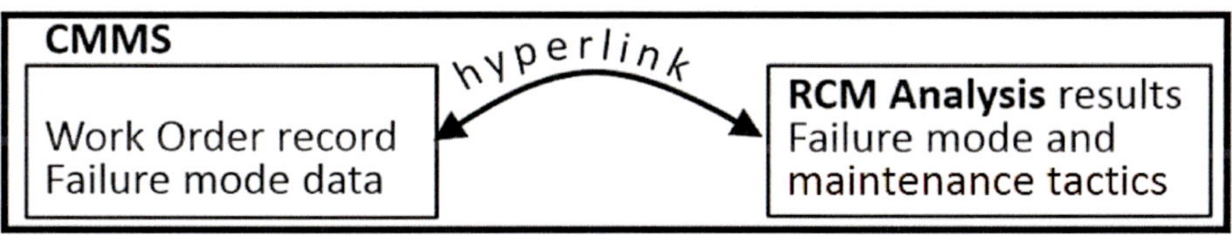

Figure 4-13: Storing RCM results in the CMMS.

Creating the RCM Application inside the CMMS

Using the standard configuration tools of a best-of-breed CMMS product, you can add a new application in a matter of days (Figure 4-14). This application might be called RCM Analysis Screen. Although RCM facilitators may build their data files in Excel, the data can be uploaded to the CMMS when finished.

Note: Any configurations are upgradeable.

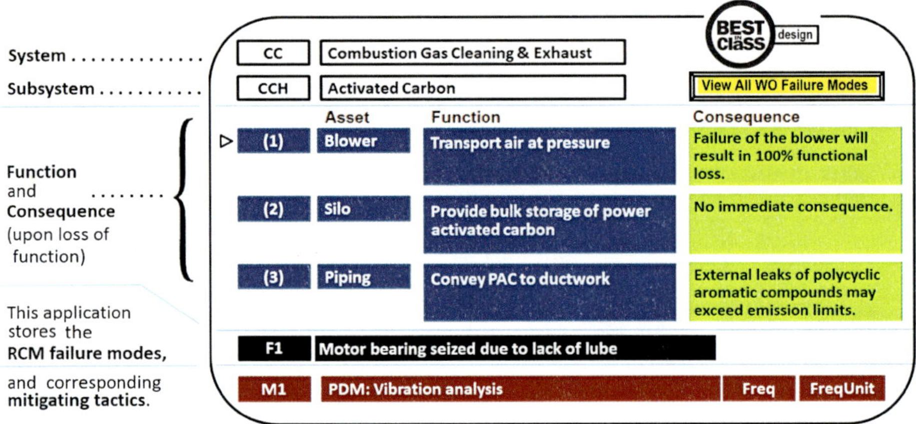

Figure 4-14: Creating the RCM application.

Benefits from an Embedded Design

The benefits of storing the results of RCM analysis inside the CMMS are substantial. Once a single work order is completed and its failure mode is captured, the maintenance engineers can quickly link that asset to the asset record in the RCM analysis screen. Furthermore, they can compare the failure modes.

If there is no entry in the RCM screen, then deploy proper procedures to insert failure modes and maintenance tactics. If there is a matching entry for the asset and failure mode, then ask "Why did this happen?" Obviously someone is needed who is qualified to perform this type of failure analysis and to have access to updates in the RCM analysis screen. There is also the role of updating the CMMS PM/PdM library to reflect changes to maintenance tactics.

Who Actually Reviews Work Order Failure Data?

Hopefully, someone reviews the Work Order failure data either as a one-off or within a Top 10 Pareto analysis (Table 4-1). Depending upon the defined roles and responsibilities, there are several different opportunities for conducting a failure analysis review, including planners, maintenance technicians, supervisors, and reliability engineers. What's important is that someone focuses on worst offenders to identify root cause.

Table 4-1: Managing Failure Data

Action	Responsibility
Enters failure data at job completion	Maintenance Technician enters failed component. Maintenance Technician enters component problem. Maintenance Technician enters Cause 1. Maintenance Supervisor enters Cause 2. Reliability Engineer enters Cause 3. Maintenance Manager conducts 1-on-1 interview to determine Cause 4 (when necessary).
Work order failure mode is new	Reliability engineer or job planner could be asked to assess new failure mode and add it to RCM analysis screen. Or the reliability team could be asked to review all new entries at end of month.
Work order failure mode is not new, but breakdown still occurred	Reliability engineers would evaluate current failure modes and suggested maintenance tactics. Then they would evaluate the associated CMMS PM/CBT records and would look at cause codes to arrive at recommendation.
Asset offender review team	This monthly meeting would be conducted by the reliability team. The overall objective is to leverage data in the CMMS, using the asset offender report, and dynamically drill down on failure modes to arrive at true cause. Once this is known, value-add recommendations can be made to minimize future occurrence.

Other Configurations to Improve Reliability

Work on the Right Asset with the Right Strategy at the Right Time

The goal of asset management is to optimize asset reliability and enhance work force productivity. Failure mode capture supports Pareto-style failure analysis. Work prioritization (along with asset criticality) is needed to schedule the right work. The combination of these programs supports proactive maintenance—and less reactive maintenance.

Many organizations manage backlog work with a simple 1-5 priority scheme where 1 is emergency, 2 is urgent, and 3–5 is routine. When two Work Orders are tied, the organization quite often goes by first-in, first-out.

The best-in-class organizations will introduce a risk-based prioritization. This is done by setting up a matrix (Figure 4-15) which merges multiple factors to arrive at a single ranking value. The ranking value is then applied to the Work Order, which allows the scheduling program to select the right work.

Different organizations set up their priorities differently. Some make priority 5 high and some make priority 1 high. Because of this variation, the matrix design allows the user to set up the importance in any direction. The desired output is the tanking value, which can be a value from 10 to 98.

With this matrix, you are applying fairness to work selection (for scheduling). This allows staff to improve work force coordination, job safety and optimize backlog reduction. It takes the guessing out of work prioritization.

	Prioritization Matrix															
Reason for Work	RFW8		RFW7		RFW6		RFW5		RFW4		RFW3		RFW2		RFW1	
Type of Work >>	Work Order				Regu-latory		Safety Env.		SchedStart Date (in range)		Operational Risk		PM / PdM TargStart Date in range		Routine (incl. MODs)	
	Emerg.		Urgent													
Asset/Loc Priority	WO Rank	Matrix PRI	WO Rank	Matrix PRI	WO Rank	Matrix PRI	WO Rank	Matrix PRI	WO Rank	Matrix PRI	WO Rank	Matrix PRI	WO Rank	Matrix PRI	WO Rank	Matrix PRI
1	98	6	88	5	78	4	68	4	58	3	48	3	38	2	26	2
2	96	6	86	5	76	4	66	3	56	3	46	3	36	2	22	1
3	94	6	84	5	74	4	64	3	54	3	44	2	34	2	18	1
4	92	6	82	5	72	3	62	3	52	2	42	2	32	1	14	1
5	90	6	80	5	70	3	60	2	50	2	40	2	30	1	10	1

Figure 4-15: Prioritization Matrix.

Implement Formal Work Order Feedback

It is commonly recognized that the employees actually working in the field have the greatest awareness of problems with assets and components. Unless management asks for their input, it may not otherwise be captured. By adding a new screen for this exact purpose, a checklist of questions can be presented at Work Order completion.

This information would then be electronically routed to the appropriate stakeholder for review/approval and action.

O&M staff may have previously shied away from feedback. Perhaps their suggestions went unheard or ignored. It is important for leadership to properly review all suggestions and respond one way or the other.

Figure 4-16 shows a sample of a Work Order feedback screen that will help capture this additional information.

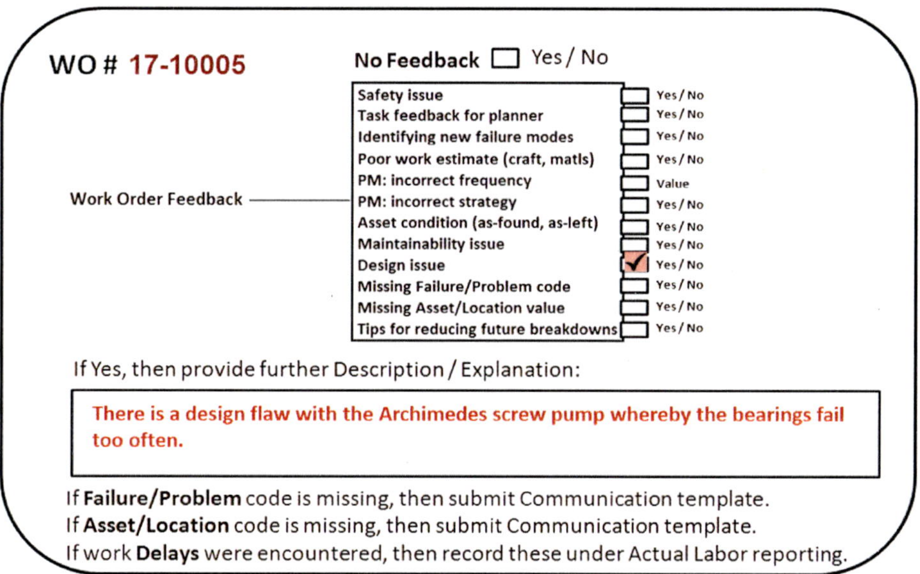

Figure 4-16: Work Order feedback screen.

Defect Tracking

With a cross-functional defect team, problems can be found and eliminated, or discussed and prioritized. What is important is that the front line workers be involved in defect identification. They have the most awareness.

Figure 4-17 supports an internationally acclaimed study by Sidney Yoshida that was initially presented in 1989 at the International Quality Symposium in Mexico City. The study indicated how management's failure to understand its processes and practices from the customers' perspective suppressed the company's profits by as much as 40 percent.

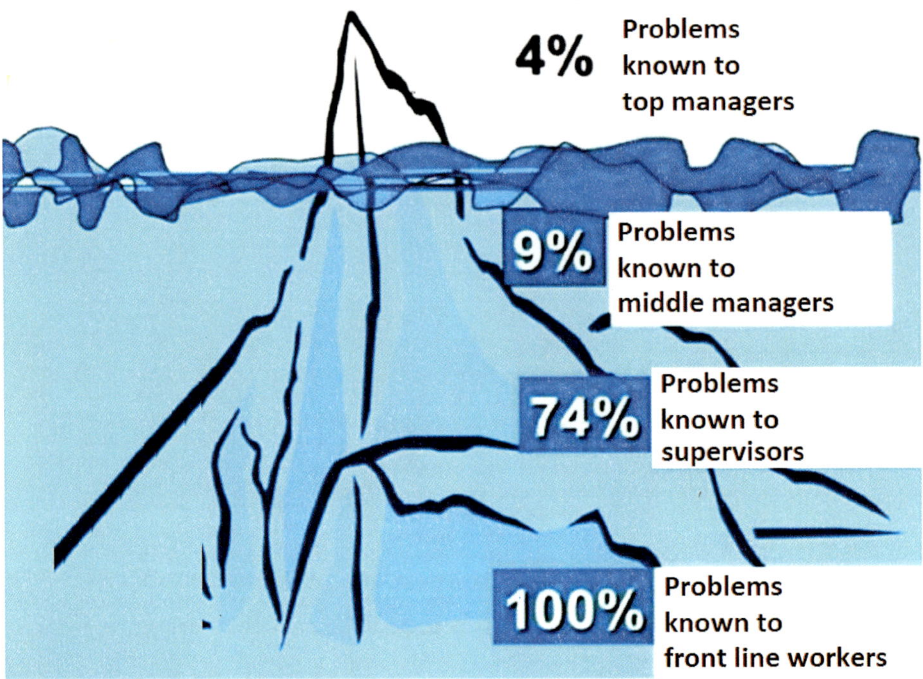

Figure 4-17: Front line employees have the greatest awareness.

Figure 4-18 shows an application you can build for the CMMS to help manage defects. It is not a Work Order, but a defect record. (It could become a Work Order.) This screen exists in the Oil and Gas Industry solution for Maximo (or Health Safety Environment extension), but could otherwise be created in the base product using configuration tools.

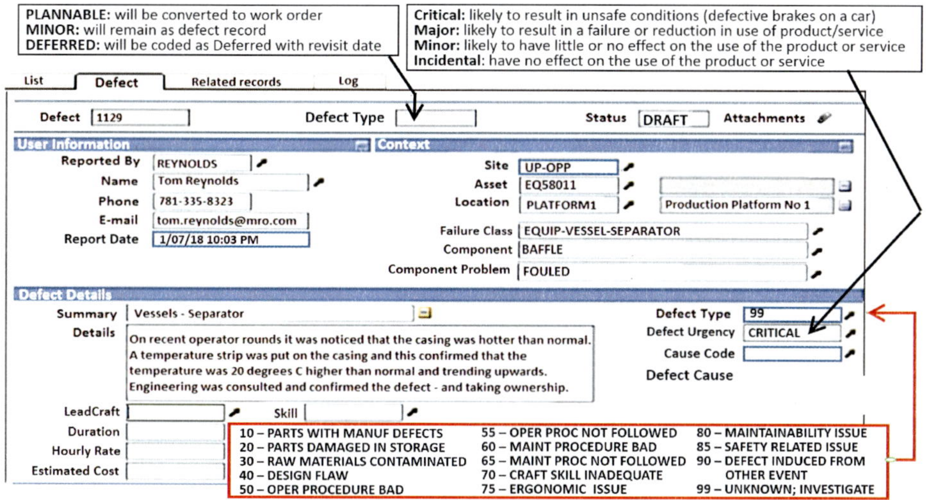

Figure 4-18: Defect record.

CHAPTER 5

Effective Asset Management

An effective asset management system has many prerequisites. By system we mean software, process, and organization. You may have certified reliability engineers in the organization, but those individuals cannot succeed by themselves. The goals must be clear, such as: 1) Enhance asset reliability, 2) Improve work force productivity, and 3) Promote job safety. By pursuing these goals, the stakeholders can start to lay out a roadmap to achieve operational excellence. As legendary football coach Vince Lombardi once said, "Perfection is not attainable, but if we chase perfection we can catch excellence."

Implement the CMMS with the End Game in Mind

Is it possible to implement asset management best practices while rolling out new CMMS software? The answer is absolutely yes, but the project team—and customer side—must have the right skill sets. These include software knowledge (requirements definition, configuration, data loading, and training) and awareness of an asset management framework such as Reliability Web or Uptime Elements. Is this asking a lot? Yes, but it is possible with the right mix of staff members.

The secret is to design the CMMS with decision making in mind. This way of thinking normally starts with an end-game definition that includes the vision/mission statement, goals/objectives, business rules, and process flow charts with swim lanes. I would take this one step further and outline analytical reports critical to business objectives. If asset reliability is a key goal, then you should have a Pareto-style failure analytic. Too many CMMS projects are predominantly software focused; they lack essential knowledge critical to asset management fundamentals.

Assuming there is an executive sponsor involved, stakeholders should sit down with them to draw up a list of improvement initiatives relating to asset management. They can then convert these initiatives into a long range plan (LRP) that links to corporate goals.

Prioritization and logic ties can be applied showing what happens first and what follows. The plan is then resource leveled to create a realistic schedule. In turn, these steps generate a critical path that tells the team where to focus. In other words, you don't half to worry about "stuff" 1–2 years from now. Periodic refinements would be made every six months.

Several roles are necessary to guarantee success:

- The core team is charged with long range planning and relies on the LRP to guide them. They should be aware of all improvement initiatives and advanced processes that support asset reliability, work force productivity, and job safety.
- The core team manages software change request, upgrades, configurations, documentation, and staff (re)training. They record actions inside a punch list.
- The business analyst—a member of the core team— manages culture. Business analysts are the first people to know if there are problems at the working level. They are also the go-between for working level and IT staff.
- The core team also develop KPIs, standard procedures, business rules, definitions, and error check routines.
- Reliability engineers (or maintenance engineers) should be aware of analytical report requirements. This design drives data inputs and process/procedure requirements.
- Conversely, without knowledge of the end game, it will take a lot longer to reach your goals.

Different Levels of Consultants

It is wise for the customer project manager to inquire as to skill sets and background of the implementation team. The different levels are shown in Figure 5-1.

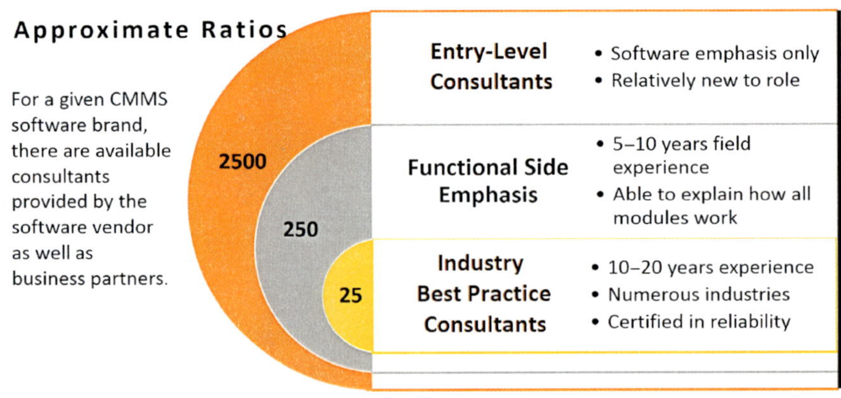

Figure 5-1: CMMS consultants.

The knowledge critical to industry best practices typically requires more than 10 years of field experience. The core team can perform benchmarking to acquire knowledge, but gaining this knowledge is an ongoing process. With the right skill sets, the project team can properly set up foundation data and start planning for advanced processes critical to return on investment. An industry best practice consultant is able to fill in for a reliability engineer and has knowledge in advanced processes critical to ROI.

Implementing Chronic Failure Analysis

Using a phased approach to this improvement initiative is ideal. This book provides detailed examples of how to set up failure codes (in support of failure mode). That said, the reliability team may want to enhance these codes to fit their industry or site.

Start Capturing Failure Mode as Soon as Possible

It is very important, however, to start capturing actionable failure data—specifically failure mode— as soon as possible. Every day that goes by is lost failure data. It is highly unlikely that you will ever go back in time and review the narrative text to create actionable data.

Designing the Ideal Failure Analytic

Take the time to draw up a design that best suits your organization. Ask the reliability engineer and others what kind of decisions they need to make. All that is required is a hand-drawn diagram during the early stages. For example, Figure 5-2 was written on a Delta airlines napkin.

Once the output requirements are known, you can identify the input requirements. You should not assume the failure analytic will be provided with out-of-the-box reports.

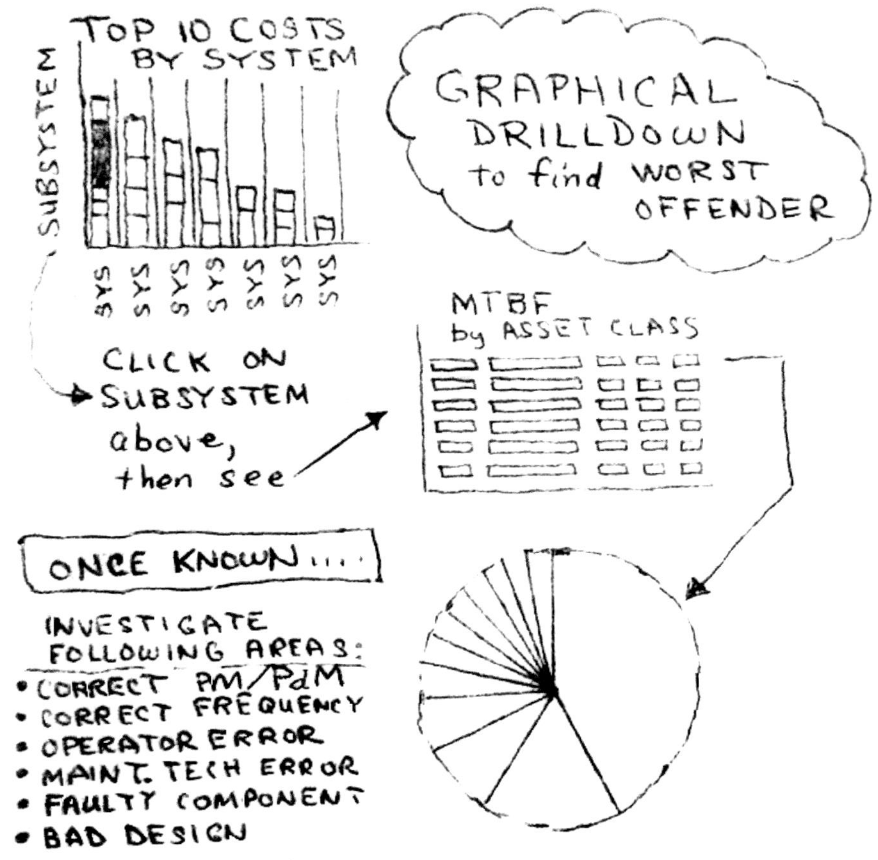

Figure 5-2: Design on a napkin!

What's More Important? The Failure Data, the Analytical Tool, or the Decision?

Face-to-face dialogue, failure data, and analytical tools are all important (Figure 5-3). But if you had to choose one, which would it be?

When decisions are required, which method do you use? Face-to-face dialog is always welcome, but is the CMMS properly configured to support value-added decision making? Some organizations focus primarily on capturing failure data. Others focus on establishing the analytical tool. But when said and done, do they make an informed decision? Do they extract knowledge from the analytic to become more proactive, to eliminate recurring issues, and to become more competitive?

Figure 5-3: Approaches to decision making.

Implementing RCM within the CMMS

Closed Loop Design Supports Ongoing Refinement

A closed loop design, as shown in Figure 5-4, is what separates the best-in-class organizations from the middle-of-the-pack. Key points include macro level review using Pareto analysis of chronic failures and the four types of Work Order feedback. Only then will an organization have a chance at achieving an 80-20 split. This is not something that can be magically mandated.

As shown, the 80-20 rule means 80% of the work is proactive work that is planned and scheduled whereas 20% is reactive with no planning or scheduling. If reactive work becomes the dominant mode, then efficiencies in reliability, productivity, and job safety will be impacted.

Other nuances to this best-in-class design include:

- Failure mode capture on the work order
- Asset offender report (Pareto-style failure analytic that allows for dynamic drill-down on failure mode)

- RCM analysis results screen inside the CMMS
- A reliability team to perform chronic failure analysis
- Defect tracking

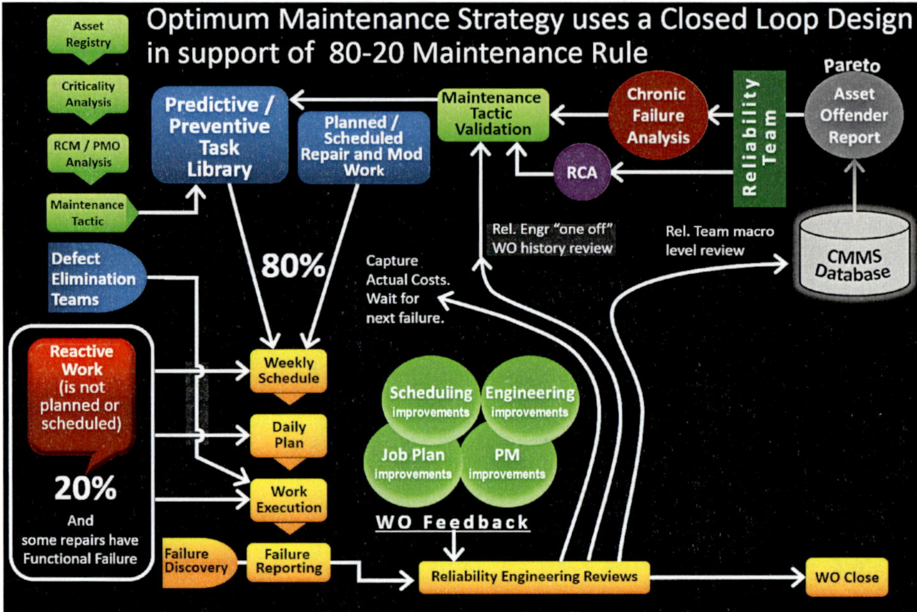

Figure 5-4: CMMS closed loop maintenance.

Reliability Team Leverages Data for Decision Making

Wouldn't it be great if you could leverage data in the CMMS to make more informed decisions? This is the job of the reliability team. Once a month, they should meet (Figure 5-5) to run the asset offender report to identify bad actors (assets) and then drill down on failure modes.

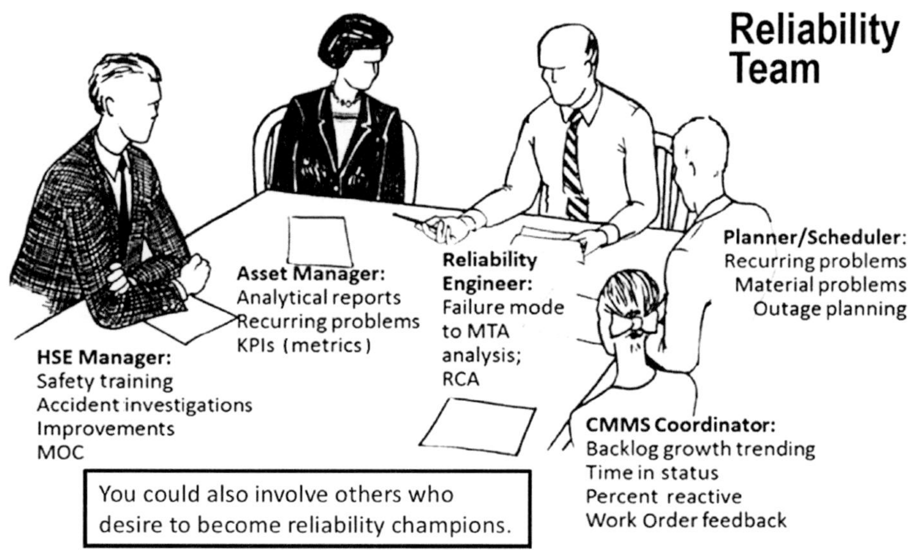

Figure 5-5: Reliability team.

Any organization that is serious about operational excellence needs stakeholders with analytical capabilities. They discuss any topic relating to asset reliability. Some examples include:

1. Apply a failure analytic design.
2. Ask about the status of the defect elimination teams and last month's success.
3. Initiate RCA where warranted based on trigger points; assign responsibility and deadlines.
4. Review emergency and urgent breakdowns from last week and ask why.
5. Ask planners to discuss significant feedback from trades on work performed that week.
6. Evaluate assets where the asset condition is trending downwards—as captured during PM activities.
7. Review engineering recommendations to update RCM analysis.
8. In regards to the weekly schedule and compliance therein, discuss "reason no-start."
9. Review time-in-status report; and look for outliers.
10. Review and trend backlog growth.
11. Discuss new condition based maintenance (CBM) work orders created by the CBT tech.
12. Discuss notes from Kaizen forums or quality circles involving operators; share observations and insights.

13. Track progress against the long range plan.
14. Continue to encourage all forms of benchmarking as well as CRL accreditation.

RCM Screen Links Failure Modes to Maintenance Tactics

Many organizations have never performed an RCM analysis (Figure 5-6). Or, they have performed this exercise just for one area, system, or asset class. Either way, with the embedded CMMS RCM application, you can now store failure information as it is discovered. For example, a failure mode might be captured at job completion. Then, once it is checked against the RCM results screen, it is discovered that this failure mode is missing.

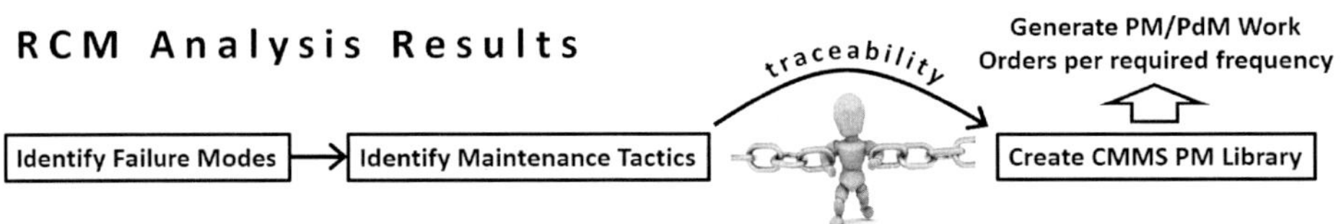

Figure 5-6: RCM analysis results.

The significance of Figure 5-7 is that the organization may have never performed RCM or PMO analysis due to a variety of reasons. But with this design, they can start capturing failure modes in an appropriate "location" within the CMMS product for ready access. Option 3 in the figure supports an RCM "build as you go" design. All that's required is staff to be trained on both RCM analysis and where to store results inside the CMMS.

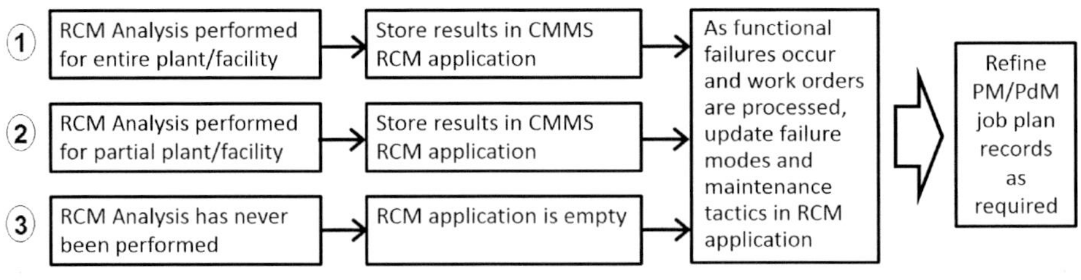

Figure 5-7: Determining a path forward regarding RCM analysis.

This Holistic Approach Blends RCM with CMMS

The Key Is Continuous Refinement

This design clearly supports the storage of RCM analysis results within the CMMS (Figure 5-8). With the right product, configuring screens should not be that hard. The toughest challenge will be adjusting to new data input requirements. In most cases, the failure mode information is known but stored in free format text. The difference here is to place this information in validated fields. Admittedly, capturing the cause codes can be challenging, but if this task is separated by role, then this detail is more likely to be captured.

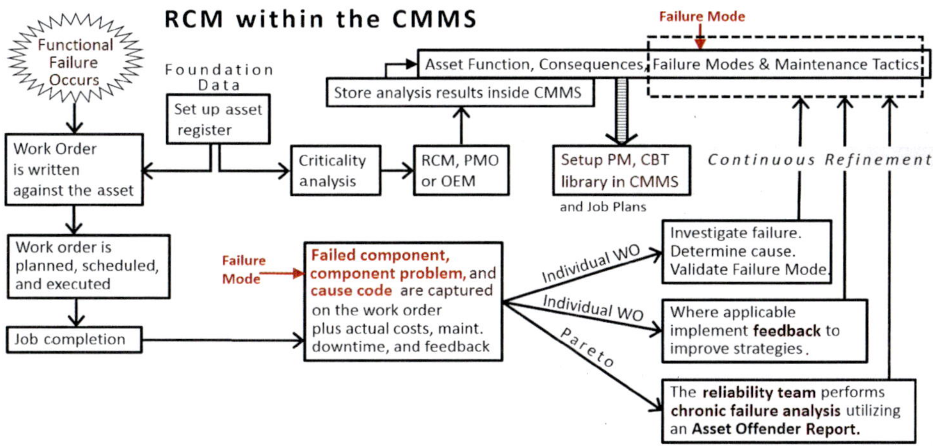

Figure 5-8: RCM within the CMMS.

A Single, Enterprise-Wide Solution Is Most Cost Effective

One software product means less software support costs. In addition, a consolidated system design is, by default, interconnected. Data moves back and forth easier. That said, there are many techniques that add value to reliability excellence (Figure 5-9). Each of these applications could be within the CMMS.

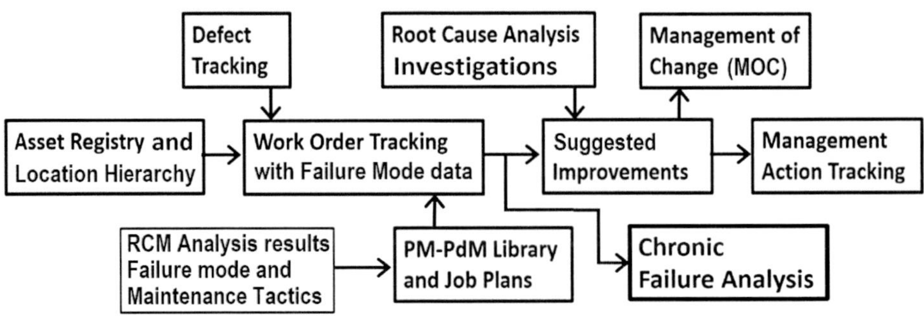

Figure 5-9: A single, enterprise-wide solution.

Pennies on the Dollar

What you now have is an affordable, build-as-you-go design for RCM analysis with easy data update—making this entire process and design a true "living program." The best RCM analysis is one where the results can be continually refined. With this program's ease-of-update, the odds are much greater that the reliability champions will continually improve the failure data and maintenance tactics. In turn, they will be able to optimize O&M costs.

Leverage CMMS to Make More Informed Decisions

In many cases, the implementation team chooses to focus on the simpler tasks such as screen configuration, report build, and data loading. They may never even involve the reliability engineer. If the failure analytic is not defined—even on paper—there is a good chance they will go live with wrong or incomplete failure data.

You can set up a CMMS to create electronic Work Orders, to track backlog growth, to issue parts, and to plan work. But if you don't have the ability to perform chronic failure analysis, you really just have a Work Order ticket system.

The CMMS database should be reliable and accurate. The foundation data should be complete and the transaction data should be both accurate and timely. Your ability to extract critical information provides you with a competitive advantage. There are three prerequisites to establishing this knowledge base:

1. Leadership should have a well-defined end game with a clear roadmap.
2. The roles should be clear.
3. The software should be configurable.

A well-informed core team will understand the fundamentals of asset management. The CMMS software can be set up to improve decision making. Advanced processes, such as chronic failure analysis, can be implemented to leverage data in the CMMS and maximize ROI. As business executive and author Jack Welch once said, "An organization's ability to learn, and translate that learning into action rapidly, is the ultimate competitive advantage." Properly designed analytical reports can be that difference maker.

Success and Sustainability

"You have to know the past to understand the present."
Carl Sagan

Carl Sagan's insight is applicable to achieving reliability excellence. Chronic failure analysis enables the stakeholders to review failure history—discovering patterns (i.e., know the past) that help them focus on worst offenders (i.e., understand the present).

Asset management success is measured by how effectively leadership can make more informed decisions based on validated data. It is also about managing by exception and learning from past problems. It's hard to fix everything at once. But, by focusing on the worst offenders, you will be spending your time and effort in the best places. As an advanced process, it has the largest potential return on investment within the asset management system.

Creating a "Build as You Go" Design

Figure 5-10 provides a comparison roadmap linking to reliability excellence. The three options are shown as red, black, and green. Each option has a different price point and level of effort. I believe the green option offers the most cost effective and creative solution.

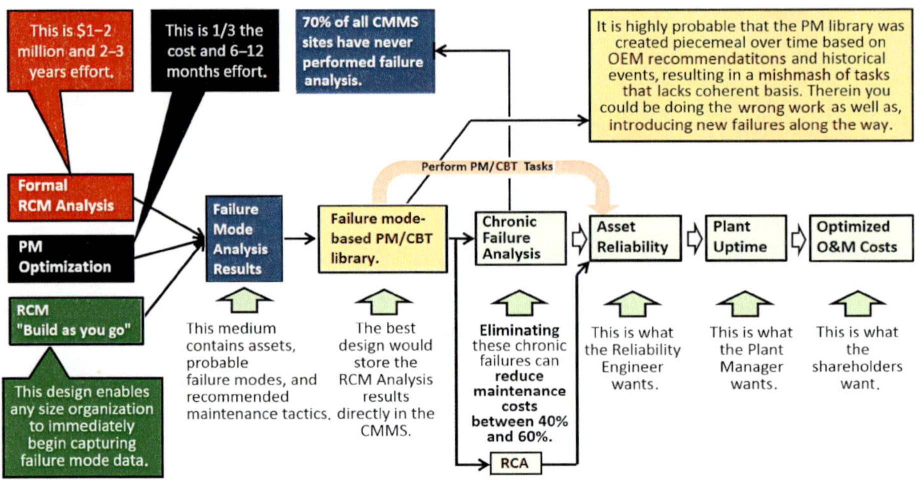

Figure 5-10: The comparison roadmap.

In Summary

Maintenance is performed at the component level. If stakeholders are to track recurring failures, shouldn't this tracking be actionable data within the CMMS? For whatever reason, the majority of all products on the market lack the capability to track failure mode. In addition, they do not understand the significance of Pareto-style failure analysis. The strategy outlined in this book provides a sure-fire way to leverage technology to make better decisions.

Every maintenance strategy listed in the CMMS preventive maintenance library should have a link back to the RCM/PMO analysis—and failure mode—that it is trying to prevent. The best way to accomplish this goal is to store the RCM analysis results directly inside the CMMS. Furthermore, with a validated failure mode, you can create a three-way match from the Work Order to the RCM analysis results screen to the preventive maintenance (PM/CBT) library.

With the Asset Offender Report in hand, a strong reliability team will be able to optimize return on asset, which is of interest to the shareholders. Lastly, chronic failure analysis empowers every organization to make value-add decisions and react to change quicker.

Although the title of the book is *Failure Modes to Failure Codes*, it could also be called *How to Implement Chronic Failure Analysis*, or, *How to Save Bundles of Money.* Without this failure mode definition, three-way match capability, and chronic failure analysis, the majority of all organizations are most likely performing maintenance they don't need to be performing.

Why Should You Care?

When senior management starts questioning the value of the CMMS, they will point to a lack of failure data and failure analytics as well as the cost of operating. The working level may also reach a tipping point and "turn against the system." The next thing you know, someone wants to purchase new software.

> Organizations that lack a strong understanding in asset management principles usually place too much emphasis on the software, thinking it will singlehandedly improve asset reliability and plant uptime.
>
> A business analyst will be the first person to know that culture is bad and a tipping point has been reached. Do you have a business analyst?
>
> Thousands of articles exist on the internet discussing bad data and weak reports. Chronic failure analysis offers the best chance to improve decision making and optimize O&M costs—using the CMMS.
>
> All that's required is a vision for excellence and a roadmap to get there.

ABOUT THE AUTHORS

John Reeve

John Reeve was the second consultant hired by the company that invented Maximo. He spent the first ten years as an international consultant in project management involving scheduling system and cost management design. Aerospace and defense industries as well as nuclear power plant construction and operation depended on this software. In the following 20 years, his focus shifted to asset management design. During this time, he submitted a U.S. Patent in maintenance scheduling for an "order of fire" design. He can comfortably discuss advanced processes for both asset reliability and work force productivity. These combined field experiences plus certified reliability leader accreditation have created a framework from which to share valuable insight.

His credentials include 12,000 LinkedIn followers, 100 postings on industry best practices, numerous trade magazine articles, and this book, *Failure Modes to Failure Codes*. His combined knowledge in both project management and asset management make him unique in the consulting field. His goal is to bring the CMMS community closer to the world of RCM practitioners. Significant overseas assignments included Australian Defence Industry (Sydney), Australian Submarine Corporation (Adelaide), Pohang Steel (South Korea), and Power Generation Company of Trinidad.

ABOUT THE AUTHORS

Derek Burley CRL, CMRP, MIAM

Derek spent twenty years working in British Rail signaling as a control and systems engineer. In 1997, he moved to the United States, working as an Asset Management and RCM consultant across a wide range of industries: oil & gas (O&G), railroad, food, automobile, cement production, wastewater treatment, mining (copper and diamonds), and pharma and medical. In 2003, he joined Cargill and was engaged in establishing RCM training programs, facilitation certification, and standards development. In 2008, he moved to Rio Tinto as Principal Advisor—Maintenance Tactics Development, based in Salt Lake City, Utah.

Over the last 15 years, he has presented papers, articles, and workshops at numerous conferences on a variety of subjects including RCM, human error, change management, reliability engineering, asset management, and procedure based maintenance. He founded Blue Sky Reliability Consulting LLC in 2013. The company specializes in asset management and RCM training, facilitation services, and project support.

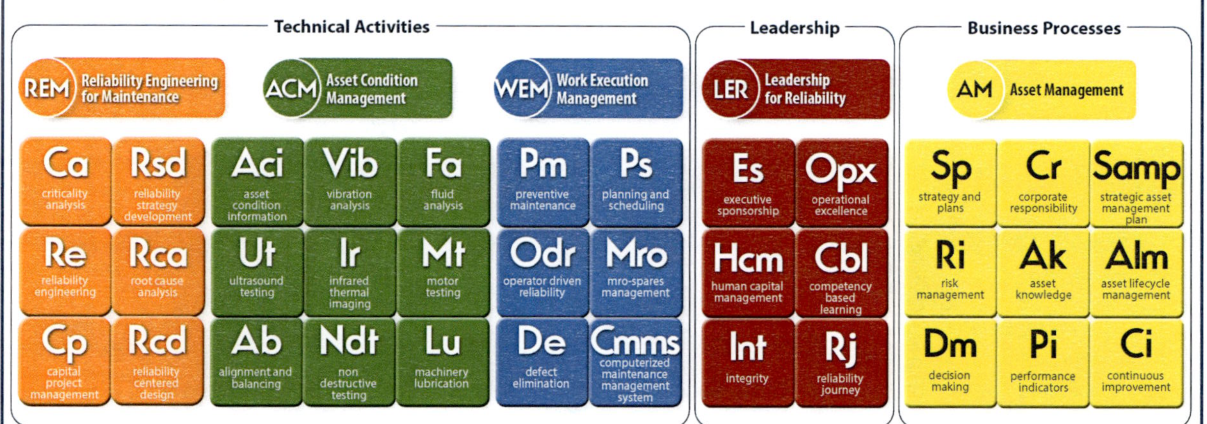

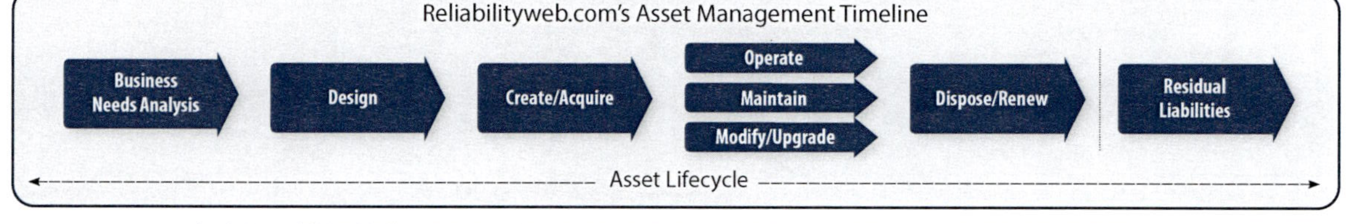

reliabilityweb.com • maintenance.org • reliabilityleadership.com

Reliabilityweb.com® and Uptime® Magazine Mission: **To make the people we serve safer and more successful.** One way we support this mission is to suggest a reliability system for asset performance management as pictured above. Our use of the Uptime Elements is designed to assist you in categorizing and organizing your own Body of Knowledge (BoK) whether it be through training, articles, books or webinars. Our hope is to make YOU safer and more successful.

ABOUT RELIABILITYWEB.COM

Created in 1999, Reliabilityweb.com provides educational information and peer-to-peer networking opportunities that enable safe and effective reliability and asset management for organizations around the world.

ACTIVITIES INCLUDE:

Reliabilityweb.com® (www.reliabilityweb.com) includes educational articles, tips, video presentations, an industry event calendar and industry news. Updates are available through free email subscriptions and RSS feeds. **Confiabilidad.net** is a mirror site that is available in Spanish at www.confiabilidad.net.

Uptime® Magazine (www.uptimemagazine.com) is a bi-monthly magazine launched in 2005 that is highly prized by the reliability and asset management community. Editions are obtainable in both print and digital.

Reliability Leadership Institute® Conferences and Training Events (www.reliabilityleadership.com) offer events that range from unique, focused-training workshops and seminars to small focused conferences to large industry-wide events, including the International Maintenance Conference (IMC), MaximoWorld and The RELIABILITY Conference™ (TRC).

MRO-Zone Bookstore (www.mro-zone.com) is an online bookstore offering a reliability and asset management focused library of books, DVDs and CDs published by Reliabilityweb.com.

Association of Asset Management Professionals (www.maintenance.org) is a member organization and online community that encourages professional development and certification and supports information exchange and learning with 50,000+ members worldwide.

A Word About Social Good

Reliabilityweb.com is mission-driven to deliver value and social good to the reliability and asset management communities. *Doing good work and making profit is not inconsistent*, and as a result of Reliabilityweb.com's mission-driven focus, financial stability and success has been the outcome. For over a decade, Reliabilityweb.com's positive contributions and commitment to the reliability and asset management communities have been unmatched.

Other Causes

Reliabilityweb.com has financially contributed to include industry associations, such as SMRP, AFE, STLE, ASME and ASTM, and community charities, including the Salvation Army, American Red Cross, Wounded Warrior Project, Paralyzed Veterans of America and the Autism Society of America. In addition, we are proud supporters of our U.S. Troops and first responders who protect our freedoms and way of life. That is only possible by being a for-profit company that pays taxes.

I hope you will get involved with and explore the many resources that are available to you through the Reliabilityweb.com network.

Warmest regards,
Terrence O'Hanlon
CEO, Reliabilityweb.com